THE LAID
GUIDE TO EXAMS and STRESS

BY

Jennie Caswell

and Naseem Ahsun

Illustrated by Rodge David

Published by Motivational Press, Inc.
1777 Aurora Road
Melbourne, Florida, 32935

www.MotivationalPress.com

Illustrated by Rodge David

Manufactured in the United States of America.

ISBN: 978-1-62865-275-8

CONTENTS

DEDICATION

We dedicate this book to all of you, who are currently studying for your exams and experiencing stress.

We also dedicate this book to the beautiful connections that surround us in our world, especially the connections with our animal guides and their psychic, subtle guidance to us, their human friends.

Our animal guides invite us to pause in our frantic, stressful lives and connect with our natural higher-selves.

ACKNOWLEDGEMENT

Our beautiful book demonstrates how marvellous support is around all of us in each and every moment.

Rodge David, our inspirational illustrator, has brought the animal clan guides to life with his natural magic and strength. His intuitive ability to channel the animals into drawings has opened the door for everyone to connect with their animal clan guide and his contributions have taken this book to a new level.

Also, thank you to our families for their fantastic inputs, inspirations, understanding and productive guidance:

Jaime Trumper, Daniel Meylan, Paris Ahsun Ransome-Williams and Samuel Ahsun Ransome-Williams.

To our guides who have been our friends and teachers on this journey and beyond:

Jennie extends her deepest gratitude to Gordan Law, Jennie's friend and psychotherapy supervisor and mentor. He has guided Jennie on her pathway as a psychotherapist and also guided her through her dyslexia with compassion, humour and total understanding. His commitment has inspired her to reach her goals and she wishes to give him her deepest gratitude and appreciation for all his time and effort in helping her to connect to her here and now.

Jennie also wants to thank Kate Spohrer, friend and colleague, who has given Jennie immeasurable knowledge and insight into a variety of psychotherapy practices and has always been there for her in times of need.

Naseem wants to send her deepest thanks, love and appreciation to Laurence Gouldbourne, who has been there for her in every way. His diligent proofreading skills, encouragement and care helped to make her dreams a reality.

Naseem also wants to extend her greatest respect and gratitude to Lynne Hackles, Naseem's friend and writing mentor. Her advice, wisdom, encouragement and excellent proofreading skills have helped immensely.

Without the following people and their generous assistance, the completion of this book would have been much more difficult. We thank the following people for giving up their precious time:

Jaime Trumper, Warwick Trumper Daniel Meylan, Paul Caswell, Jenni and Sue Goodwin, Paris Ahsun Ransome-Williams, Samuel Ahsun Ransome-Williams, Julia, Jade, Dylan, Yazmin, Audery, Zara, John Hancox, Sarah, John, Lilly, Vivienne and Jack.

So much goes on behind the scenes when writing a book and involves resources that come in many forms and varieties. So thanks to all those who have worked behind the scenes:

First Paige, who offered lots of suggestions around publishing and printing our affirmation cards. Your dedicated patience and tolerance was beyond the call of duty.

Sarah Ray of Design Marque who has the amazing ability to tune into our needs and wants, giving more of herself than we ever expected. She is much appreciated.

Bishop Perowne Church of England College, including: Head Teacher, Mark Pollard, Rachel Gaston, as well as Head of Performing Arts, Celia Alexander and finally to Edward Steele-Fox.

Amanda Cholko for her fantastic editing skills and suggestions, which have contributed to a clear sense of what we want to share with the world.

Deepest gratitude to Justin Sachs and Motivational Press for all their united support: your belief and faith in us and our shared values, has given us an opportunity to support teenagers and young adults in overcoming their life challenges.

Finally, we want to thank everybody who has shared and celebrated in our success.

We give hugs to you all for your belief in us, as well as our belief in you. We are all connected and are part of this great network of energy and humanity.

FOREWORD

The Laid Back Guide to Exams and Stress comes at a critical moment to support increasingly stressed teens and young adults with the relentless exam-based system they face. With an increase in stress amongst teens and young adults growing around the world, and their wellbeing at severe risk, this guide with its bespoke, insightful and practical advice offers a light in the dark world of exams and stress.

It's not so much the fact that stress is the main culprit of why teens and young adults in general fail to succeed; rather, it is that they have not been given the healthy tools to learn how to manage their stress. This is because many parents and adults are also at a loss when it comes to dealing with stress in a healthy way – so how can they teach something they've never managed to do themselves?

Even worse, there is a general misconception that teenagers and young adults are selfish and have nothing to be stressed about - a belief that their lack of motivation and disenchantment is down to their lazy attitude. However, the Laid Back Guide invites the reader to dig beneath the surface and gain a better understanding of how stress impacts on wellbeing. Discover tools that motivate, and offer an alternative to the usual model of one size fits all when it comes to dealing with exams and stress.

It offers new and insightful ways of dealing with stress in a healthy way by inviting the reader to connect with their animal clan guide who will lead them to a healthier way of handling their nerves.

Furthermore, this book is a stepping-stone in inviting the reader on a path of self-discovery – an opportunity to become more self-aware of who they are and how they can work at their optimum level to achieve the life they truly want.

Justin Sachs, CEO, Motivational Press

'The education of the heart is vital.

You must have a sense of caring for one another because the destruction of your enemies, is the destruction of yourself. Our way of life is so interconnected.'

Dalai Lama

PREFACE

Now, how many times have you experienced a churning stomach, shaking hands, or a general sense of apprehension and worry? We know we have, many times, especially when there is potential change on the horizon. Change such as attending an interview, or sitting an exam.

Do those nerves get the better of you? No matter how hard you try to ignore them, they may get bigger and bigger. Even worse, may be the constant internal chatter that doesn't have an off switch. It can get louder and louder until you can't hear anything else. You may feel this way, or have felt like this. So - those nerves - how do you handle them? How would you *like* to handle them?

We'd like to share with you now, how we have learnt to handle our nerves. Whatever the situation!

We believe that it's part of the journey of 'self-mastery' and supports our inner stability, growth and development. By learning and applying these simple techniques to our everyday existence, we open ourselves up to a choice of options that assists us in rising to our full potential.

So come with us on a journey, while we share our experiences and techniques with you.

These various techniques will be very useful in your understanding of how to approach yourself in a different way. You'll be amazed by the transformation! These techniques will help you to support yourself, particularly in times of difficulty or challenge.

Part of the process is learning to understand yourself better, as well as accept yourself completely - don't squash down bits you don't like. Don't suppress your needs; just understand all parts of yourself (your Being) without judgement and read on to discover who you really are. Discover your true, integrated potential by learning how to have different options in approaching difficult situations and challenges.

That's right! Gain the support that you truly deserve and kiss those nerves good-bye, once and for all.

Jennie Caswell and Naseem Ahsun

INTRODUCTION

DON'T PANIC

Our intention, in bringing this book to you, is to provide you with a toolbox to help you deal with your exam stress in a healthy and successful way. It's an area we feel passionately about and is based upon our own personal experience of exam stress: as students experiencing exam stress, as teachers supporting students with exam stress and as parents living with students experiencing exam stress.

We've all experienced exam stress at some point in our lives. Remember the build up to the dreaded day? Cramming as much information into your head as possible the night before, with little to no sleep. Worrying yourself sick about what was on the paper and praying your worst topic wouldn't come up. Trust us, we've been there and back again over the years.

Exam season is a time when a lot is happening – when you may feel overwhelmed and in a fog. There is a lot of external pressure, as well as the voice in your head that only increases your level of stress and, when ignored, could lead to mental health problems. You begin to feel lethargic, a loss of energy, as if you're on the verge of burning out.

Other physical symptoms might also include - headaches, upset stomach or trouble sleeping. This is because your body begins releasing high levels of cortisol and adrenalin (hormones), which is the body's automatic response if it feels under attack (e.g. the fight or flight response). Often, you find you can do neither and just freeze instead, further increasing levels of cortisol and adrenalin. This makes things even worse as your stress levels continue to rage out of control until it becomes a vicious circle. You might be someone who lets it all out, or even worse, someone who keeps it all in - silently suffering. You might put on a false air of bravado, pretending you don't care when in fact the opposite is true. Even worse, you may well just give up because you're so stressed. Whatever your response, it's a lonely and horrible place to be in.

In the UK, according to *Childline*, part of the NSPCC (National Society for the Prevention of Cruelty to Children), between April 2013 – March 2014 there has been a 200% increase in exam related stress. In particular the *Under Pressure – Childline Review (April 2013 – March 2015)* reports that:

Stresses about exams affected young people's ability to sleep, triggered anxiety attacks, depression and tearfulness, and eating disorders. In some cases it also led to self-harm and suicidal feelings, or made them worse (p. 52).

However, all is not lost. There are alternatives that are far healthier and can serve you for life, which we will explore in this book.

We hope it will empower you to break that cycle by inviting you on a journey to discover your personality type, identifying how it responds to exam stress and how you can use specific techniques that will help you managed your exam stress in a healthy way.

SO HOW DOES IT ALL WORK?

Much like a recipe, we have blended and added different viewpoints and perspectives – from philosophy to the natural world, and psychology to humanistic therapies – to bring you a unique tool that will work for you and includes: The Enneagram, Jungian Theory, Humanistic Theory and The Natural World.

WHAT IS THE ENNEAGRAM?

The Enneagram is a modern blend of old spiritual systems and contemporary psychology that encourages and supports us to connect with our real self. The word itself originates from ancient Greece (Ennea = 9 and Grammos = Figures). It describes 9 human personality types or characteristics.

Although we have all 9 energies within us, we also have a preference for one of the energy types and the Enneagram gives a detailed understanding of each energy type.

WHAT IS THE JUNGIAN SCHOOL OF THOUGHT?

Carl Jung, a 20th Century psychologist, believed that the human personality was divided up into a number of separate parts. The three main parts included: the ego, the personal unconscious and the collective unconscious. He also believed that our personalities were linked to our ancestors and also human development over time (evolution).

WHAT IS THE HUMANISTIC THEORY?

This theory encourages self-actualization, which means that we are encouraged to recognize our own capabilities, potential and creativity. It views us as a whole person, made up of many parts. Central to this theory is the idea of free will and recognising the human potential for positive growth and development. In particular, recognition of our spiritual dreams and goals are a really important part of this process. The Humanistic Theory includes areas like: Psychotherapy, Transactional Analysis, person-centred therapy and Transpersonal Psychology.

WHAT IS THE NATURAL WORLD?

Since ancient times, humanity has always sought guidance from their environment to confirm what they are sensing, and there has always been a natural affinity to the animal world. As humans, we are drawn to certain species. For example, why do some people love dogs, yet others hate them? How many of us link ourselves with an animal? Even our language provides examples of how we associate ourselves with animals: for example, 'You dirty rat'; 'stubborn mule;' 'lazy cow' or even 'sly old fox'. If you've ever studied Shakespeare, you will notice the numerous references to animals in his plays. From the ancient tales of the Werewolf to the modern tales of '*Vessan*' from the popular American TV series, like *Grimm,* we continue our close relationship with the animal kingdom.

THE ANIMAL CLAN GUIDE PERSONALITY TYPES

In this book, we have attributed an animal clan guide to each of the 9 personality types. These animal clan guides represent the energy or aura of each personality type and they resonate deeply with the particular traits associated with each type. They also help us to connect to the unseen, extrasensory world surrounding us.

YOUR GREMLIN

We all have one. It lives inside of us, constantly putting us down and undermining our confidence. Sometimes, we can sabotage ourselves by listening to our gremlin's critical voice, especially when we are experiencing stress. Later on, we will take a closer look at how our gremlin operates and how we can neutralize its impact by tapping into the gifts and tools offered by our animal clan guides.

HOW TO USE THIS BOOK

You will have to decide which animal clan guide represents your personality type so you can receive the appropriate guidance for your personality type. It is important to note that no animal or personality type is better than the other, so go with your gut instinct, versus your mental preference. The nine animal-personality types you will be choosing from are:

The Swan channels an aura of grace and elegance.

The Dog channels an aura of faithfulness and generosity.

The Lioness channels an aura of dignity and tenacity.

The Wolf channels an aura of mystique and mystery.

The Tiger channels an aura of the wise, solitary observer.

The Deer channels an aura of nurturing care and loyalty.

The Otter channels an aura of playful jubilance.

The Bear channels an aura of courageous strength and fierce protectiveness.

The Orangutan channels an aura of relaxed ease.

Try to decide on which one feels familiar. Remember that the first choice is usually the right one. Then that animal clan guide will show you a new way to approach your problems in your life. Having established your connection with your animal clan guide, go to the relevant chapter and find out how they are going to show you a new, healthy way of dealing with exam stress.

Now, let's see if your intuition is correct by taking the animal clan guide quiz at the back of the book, Appendix 1. If your quiz results differ from your initial choice, then read both and decide which one best represents you.

'Excellence does not require perfection'

Henry James

CHAPTER 1

THE SWAN

MY IDEAL WORLD

I want the world to be a better place where everything is perfect and nobody makes mistakes.

HOW I SEE THE REAL WORLD

I get so fed up sometimes because I can't be who I really want to be. Everyone expects me to be perfect *all of the time.* If I make a mistake, or step out of line, I am judged, criticised and even punished for it. I'm my own worst critic. Even when people tell me I'm doing ok, I don't believe them because my inner critic won't let me.

HOW I COPE WITH LIFE

I have learned that by being good, responsible and doing things the right way, which means I *always* follow the rules, I can keep my inner-critic happy because I have maintained my high expectations. Unfortunately, this often means that I have to suppress my anger and not let it escape. Therefore, I can come across as overly sensitive and grumpy because I can get tense and irritable as I can't say or do what I really want to.

KEY CHARACTERISTICS

I am

- Honest and uphold my strong moral principles.
- A Perfectionist.
- A Hard-worker.
- Imaginative and creative.
- Self-reliant and able to cope.
- In control of myself.
- Shy.
- Highly responsible because I can be depended on.

WHAT I HATE DEALING WITH

- Making mistakes.
- Losing self-control.
- Breaking any rules, especially in a social situation.
- Feeling flawed, bad or being wrong.

HOW I THINK AND BEHAVE

- I think that people should follow the rules and behave in an appropriate manner.

- I judge how I am doing by judging how other people are behaving.
- I criticize myself and think that others always criticize me.

WHAT I DON'T SEE

- It's never as simple as being right, or wrong. Sometimes, it's not that straightforward; there is also the grey area in-between right and wrong.
- The difference between being motivated and wanting to act, compared to acting impulsively.

HOW I COMMUNICATE

- Being precise, clear and direct.
- There is always a judgement in everything that I say, which is either right or wrong.
- Others see me as overly judgemental, critical, limiting and close-minded.

HOW I RESPOND TO EXAM STRESS

I become really anxious and worried because my inner critic gets louder and louder. It tells me, 'I am not good enough, I am hopeless and a bad person'. Eventually, the voice gets so loud and too much for me that I find it extremely hard to cope and I become overwhelmed. I also get really, really angry because I feel so useless and I turn that anger onto myself, instead of redirecting it toward structuring my studying and exam study schedule. This is because I feel that there is too much information to learn and I will not be able to learn everything perfectly, so why bother! I begin to exaggerate everything, making it more terrible and bigger than it actually is and I become melodramatic. I'll get an Oscar for throwing a tantrum or breaking down in tears.

Really, it's no one's fault, it's only because I'm scared and frightened. Frightened of my parents', carers' and teachers' expectations – what if I fail them? What will they say? What will they do? It will all be my own fault because I'm not good enough and I've let everybody else down. At this stage, all my dreams are broken and I really don't want to deal with the real world anymore.

THE TOOLS I CAN USE TO DEAL WITH EXAM STRESS

- Create a vision board full of my dreams and aspirations.
- Recognise my unrealistic expectations by not pushing myself too hard.
- Focus on reality by listing my priorities for the week, including doing an exam study schedule.
- Include regular fun-filled activities whilst I'm studying. Mark this on my exam study schedule.
- Explore others' viewpoints about how they approach exams.
- Remind myself that all the work I've done is enough.
- Avoid using the word **'should'** in my vocabulary. Instead, change it to **'can'** e.g. 'I **should** do these exams perfectly', will become, 'I **can** do these exams perfectly.'
- Remember that there are lots of ways to solve a problem, not just one way.
- Remember to do something creative such as: cooking, dancing, music or art and build that in every day.
- Focus on what I've done right versus what's wrong.
- Avoid using food, alcohol or drugs to escape my anxiety.
- Think of three things I am grateful for EVERY MORNING.
- Find something beautiful in my room and focus on it.

- Observe how a swan copes with life and think about the message it gives me.

STUDY TIPS

- I'm a bit of a workaholic and forget to take breaks. It's only when I develop physical symptoms, like headaches or stomach aches, that I realise I'm overdoing it.
- It's really important for me to have fun whilst studying, so I need to build in some fun time doing things I love and that help me to relax.
- When I'm stuck, I must seek answers from my teachers straight away, instead of sitting and worrying about it.
- Bullet pointing the facts for each subject/topic and creating a fact file really works for me.
- Having a wild dance in my bedroom is the best form of releasing all that tension I tend to carry around.
- Getting some fresh air and reconnecting with the real world is a good way for me to come back to reality.
- I really need to remind myself that I am ok and that everything is on schedule.
- Avoid spending ages trying to do everything perfectly and remind myself that good enough is good enough.

LEARNING STYLES

I am an effective learner when

- I take responsibility to structure and take control of my workload.
- I take lots of notes in class and listen very carefully to what the teacher is saying.
- I feel valued by the teacher and others in the class.

- The teacher stays on track.
- I know the rules of the classroom.
- Things are neat and tidy.
- I have a harmonious environment that is not too hot, or not too cold.
- I can learn in a logical and sequential way, breaking things down into smaller chunks.

GETTING SUPPORT FROM OTHERS

What would you say to your parents, carers and teachers who want to support you?

- Please remind me to not be so hard on myself and drop my ridiculously high standards. I tend to think that I've got to do everything now, versus do things on another day.
- I'd be really grateful if you could remind me that it is ok to take my time and that breaking down bigger tasks into small realistic steps will help me complete all tasks. I don't do very well when under pressure and people are telling me that I'm not trying hard enough.
- Lots of patience and non-judgemental feedback really helps to relax and de-stress me.
- Humour goes a long way too, as it encourages me to have fun.
- Tell me it's ok for me to make mistakes as it reminds me that I'm human. Also, encourage me to stop and have fun during my exam preparation, so it doesn't seem like a prison sentence.
- Please help me to let go of things I can't change or control by reminding me to stay in the moment and not dwell on the past.
- Coax me to focus on what I have achieved in a day versus what I have not.

- If I become demotivated and throw in the towel, please remind me to stop my 'stinky thinking' and remind me that if I structure my time, all will be well because I will have a balance of work and fun.

AFFIRMATIONS TO HELP ME STAY ON TRACK

I remind myself that I am good enough and everything is unfolding perfectly.

Now, I treat myself with love and tenderness and value my perfections.

NB. For more affirmations, see details about the *Laid Back Guide Affirmation Cards* in the Appendices.

REMEMBER -

The Swan invites you to accept that you have its natural grace, serene inner beauty and can manage life's challenges in a swan-like way. Remind yourself of how the swan is able to appear to glide through life effortlessly.

The Swan is graceful and serene, so it invites you to connect with your inner gift of calmness and what you do well. Remember, you are very powerful and succeed at most things. And you will create your own perfection in your world that is good enough.

'Never allow someone else to be your priority while allowing yourself to be an option'

Mark Twain

CHAPTER 2

THE DOG

MY IDEAL WORLD

I would love to see a place where everything and everyone is equal and cared for.

HOW I SEE THE REAL WORLD

I believe that I am not liked for just me. People only like me, or want to be around me when I can be useful to them. Ultimately, I am a resource.

HOW I COPE WITH LIFE

I love giving to people because it makes me feel needed and wanted. By being helpful, I become useful and people will not want to get rid of me, so I tend to do an awful lot of favours for other people in all areas of my life. I'm a great friend to have around because I'll always be there for you, even when it's not convenient.

KEY CHARACTERISTICS

I am

- Full of praise and always complimenting others.
- Really giving and generous.
- Sensitive to how others are feeling.
- Love to help.
- A complete romantic.
- Caring and nurturing.
- Thoughtful and kind.

WHAT I HATE DEALING WITH

- Letting others down.
- Being taking for granted and not appreciated.
- Unkind and uncaring people.
- My own repressed needs.
- An unsupportive environment.
- Being overwhelmed by everyone's wants and needs.

HOW I THINK AND BEHAVE

- My main objective in life is to discover how I can please other people. When I meet their needs, it makes me really happy because other people feel cared for.

- Pleasing others by meeting their needs makes me feel really liked and accepted.
- Learning the rules of love and romance is my key focus, so I learn how to be a lovable, loyal partner as well as a lovable, faithful friend.

WHAT I DON'T SEE

- Is that I might be interfering with other people's personal lives.
- Is that I am not always needed and I can get in the way, sometimes.

HOW I COMMUNICATE

- With a relaxed, friendly, open and warm persona.
- I am more interested in finding out about the other person.
- I love to discover how I can support you.

HOW I RESPOND TO EXAM STRESS

I am more focused on how I can please other people, especially my teachers and parents. If I really like the teacher, then I will do well in their subject/topic because it's the best way of me becoming their favourite pupil. However, if I don't like a teacher, then you can forget it – I won't really bother with their subject.

If I have a strong bond with someone – like a parent, teacher, tutor or friend, then I will try hard to be like him or her because this is another way for me to gain approval and be wanted.

However, I tend to do things at the last minute because I think I have more time than I actually have. Often this leads me to panic and feel overwhelmed. This means that I can stay up all night and ignore my needs for sleep because I've left everything to the last minute – usually, because I've been too busy helping all my other friends with the stress of their exams.

At this stage, I will tend to turn to food, especially chocolate and junk food for comfort.

The worst possible thing to occur during the exam period is if I fall out with my partner or best friend, which causes me to feel like my world has fallen apart.

THE TOOLS I CAN USE TO DEAL WITH EXAM STRESS

- Make a list of my hopes and dreams.
- Focus on what I can achieve by being successful in my exams.
- Learn to put my needs first by saying no to others.
- Watch an inspiring film that shows someone being successful in achieving his or her objective.
- Don't sabotage my own exam study schedule for others (e.g. a friend having a crisis).
- Schedule free time with friends around my studying, not the other way around.
- Turn my phone off, so my friends don't distract me. (I know that I might find this hard to do).
- Don't rescue other people every time they cry for help.
- Regular grounding meditation, or journaling, for 15 minutes every day will help to keep me focused.
- Be mindful of my body – look after myself and avoid exhaustion by pacing myself. This is how I will remain in a positive space with myself and others.

STUDY TIPS

- Create a calming study zone in my room, or a space in my home, that is strictly for studying.

- Working in a study group is brilliant for me, so organise a study afternoon or morning with 1 or 2 friends; however, remember that I am there for MY own learning, not to rescue them.
- Write a personal creative story about a topic as a way to study and remember it.
- Focus on my most passionate subject first because it will get me into a study routine.
- When I'm tense, have some time to play chess, or a strategy game, against another person. It will take away some of the tension and also help me maintain a level of focus, too.
- Focus on the bigger picture and what I will gain from passing the subject, which will prevent me from becoming disengaged from studying.
- Make an exam study schedule and stick to it.
- I need to keep a careful eye on the balance of studying and fun time e.g. 50/50, not 20/80.
- Find out what is my best time of day to study and stick to it.
- Learn how to prioritise my subjects.

LEARNING STYLES

I am an effective learner when

- I'm given lots of praise and encouragement because it makes me feel good about myself.
- I feel useful and wanted - so if you encourage me to be a buddy for someone else, it will make me try even harder in your lessons.
- Teachers are passionate about their subject and can present it in a creative way.
- Teachers let me know how I am doing on a regular basis because

it prevents my insecurity.

- I'm involved with group discussion; it really helps me to learn.
- I am reminded to stay on target.

GETTING SUPPORT FROM OTHERS

What would you say to your parents, carers and teachers who want to support you?

- Please encourage me to be independent and become my own person versus a caricature of one of you or someone else.
- Because I am so scared of being rejected, I tend to help other people, especially friends, even when it could ruin my own chances of success, so I'd be really grateful if you can teach me how to say 'no'.
- Encourage me to focus on the bigger picture and my exam study schedule rather than always wanting to socialise. I can get lost in my friends' lives and problems to the detriment of myself.
- Please remind me to ask for what I want and to connect with what I want and what I need.
- Encourage me to get enough sleep and to eat healthily.
- Praise me for the work that I do; especially when I am being focused and sticking to my new exam study schedule. I'd really like for people to share how proud they are of me.

AFFIRMATIONS TO HELP ME STAY ON TRACK

I remind myself that I do not have to be useful to be lovable or loved.

I affirm that it is ok for me to take care of my own needs first, without feeling guilty.

NB. For more affirmations, see details about the *Laid Back Guide Affirmation Cards* in the Appendices.

REMEMBER

The Dog reminds you that your first and foremost loyalty is to YOURSELF. You are deserving of all the time, attention and praise that you give to others. When you love yourself, others will love you. It is ok to be yourself and know that everyone will love you for yourself, not who you think you need to be.

The Dog also reminds you that you are an important member of the pack, and therefore by being yourself, you serve the pack. You have a level of determination and inner strength that you can always tap into to help you deal with challenges that come your way.

'Look inside yourself, you are more than what you have become'.

Mufasa's Ghost – The Lion King

CHAPTER 3

THE LIONESS

MY IDEAL WORLD

There is no need to panic because there is a natural order to things. It is a place where everything unfolds naturally; such as, the Sun rising in the east and setting in the west. Day follows night.

HOW I SEE THE REAL WORLD

What you put in is what you get out of life. I believe that the harder I work, the more attention I get from other people because I impress them with how effective and efficient I am. It is the only way for me to receive any love, or recognition.

HOW I COPE WITH LIFE

Since I really want to be approved of, I will constantly present an efficient, confident and 'can do' image. I excel at wearing masks and hiding my true feelings, even from myself. I'm really very competitive and will work hard to be the best.

KEY CHARACTERISTICS

I am

- Competitive and have to be #1.
- Goal and task-orientated.
- I focus on the future.
- Efficient.
- Quick, easy solutions.
- Image conscious.
- A doer.
- Confident and outgoing.
- Adaptable.
- Able to read situations and people.

WHAT I HATE DEALING WITH

- Ditherers or people who are unsure of what they want.
- Being overshadowed by anyone else.
- Being made to feel vulnerable.
- Hate dealing with negative emotions such as sadness, fear or anger.
- Sitting still.
- Feeling stupid and helpless.

HOW I THINK AND BEHAVE

- I'm very organised and am excellent at organising everything and everyone. I believe that everybody needs to be organised.
- It's really important that I receive recognition for any work that I have done.
- I'm very adaptable to different situations and other people's expectations.
- I'm really good at promoting myself and other people.

WHAT I DON'T SEE

- Failure.
- Are deep feelings, which I find extremely uncomfortable - I will distract myself from feeling them.
- My unrealistic expectations.

HOW I COMMUNICATE

- Clear and concise.
- Direct and very focused.
- Extremely confident and eloquent communicator.
- Can be impatient.
- Poor listening skills when others communicate with me.
- I want to convince others of my views.

HOW I RESPOND TO EXAM STRESS

I put on my exam head, which means that on the surface I appear to be cool, calm and collected. This is because I've stuffed all my real emotions into a box and locked it. What I'm really feeling is vulnerable and scared, but I refuse to admit it. Consequently, I may well begin to suffer physically; for example, irritability or migraines. Also, when I'm not doing as well as I expect to be doing, I become really withdrawn.

I tend to focus on the subjects I am doing well in and put subjects that I struggle with on the backburner. This is because I hate admitting that I'm not good at something. However, this also means that I do not prepare for those subjects/topics thoroughly. I always check out how my friends are progressing with their studying, and if they are doing better than me, I'll compete with them.

Finally, I really love to structure my time and know exactly where and when the exam is - time, place and date.

THE TOOLS I CAN USE TO DEAL WITH EXAM STRESS

- Make an exam study schedule.
- Begin identifying subjects/topics I struggle with first versus giving up on them.
- Get a clear idea of what I want and need to do, versus focusing on impressing other people.
- Be realistic in setting boundaries for my study time.
- Have realistic expectations of myself.
- Don't cram and over-burn.
- Keep a journal, so I can express how I really feel.
- Slow down and take my time to get to grips with the detail.
- Pamper myself.
- Stop ignoring my feelings.
- Walking will help me to de- stress – make sure I walk at least once a day during exam time.

STUDY TIPS

- Study groups are excellent for me because I can motivate others and this will motivate me.
- Studying at a slower pace versus skimming subjects/topics means that I can get to grips with the detail and subject matter better.
- Summarise key concepts on post cards really helps me to recall subject matter.
- Mind maps and diagrams.
- Use lots of colour.
- Set myself a challenge each day by creating a list of topics to be done; however, keep it realistic, so choose between two to three.
- Get someone to test me on how much I have retained.
- Remember to reward myself each day; e.g. watch a film, read a book, go see a friend.

LEARNING STYLES

I am an effective learner when

- I am given clear feedback on how well I have done and what I can do to improve.
- Information is structured logically.
- The teacher communicates in a clearly focused way.
- There are clear boundaries in the classroom.
- There are rewards.
- Given concrete examples for concepts and theories.
- High-achieving environments.
- Clear objectives.

GETTING SUPPORT FROM OTHERS

What would you say to your parents, carers and teachers who want to support you?

- Please give me recognition for me, not on what I achieve.
- Encourage me to understand that I don't have to be first in everything (it's ok for me to fail and ok for me to spend some time alone).
- I don't have to be the star all of the time.
- I feel the only way for me to gain approval is to be performing all the time and doing things to impress my teachers, parents or carers. Please remind me that it is ok for me to stop, take the mask off and relax.
- Please listen to me when I talk about my feelings instead of trying to solve it for me. I find it very difficult to speak about feelings and if you encourage me to find a solution, I'll simply bury what I'm really feeling.
- Please show some care for me versus what I have achieved for you.
- Remind me to slow down, and take time out to just enjoy the day.
- Please do not compare me to other people; especially my friends when it comes to studying.
- I'd value your support to help me to refocus myself on what I want, instead of what other people expect.

AFFIRMATIONS TO HELP ME STAY ON TRACK

I am more than enough, just being myself.

I can stand still long enough and accept the care and love that others give me.

NB. For more affirmations, see details about the *Laid Back Guide Affirmation Cards* in the Appendices.

REMEMBER -

The Lioness reminds you that you are a very powerful presence just by being you. People notice you come into a room before you even do anything. You are a born leader who has the ability to respond and organise the pride.

She also teaches you how to be part of a group just by being you and shows you how to achieve your goal efficiently and effectively. You also have the ability to build on your strengths by adapting to your environment.

The Lioness has the perfect balance between action and inaction, knowing when to strike and how to conserve its strength. You are much stronger than you think you are, so recognise that your emotions are a strength, not a weakness. You are really good with making tough decisions because you follow your heart.

'Don't ever mistake my silence for ignorance, my calmness for acceptance, or my kindness for weakness.'

Anon

CHAPTER 4

THE WOLF

MY IDEAL WORLD

I believe we are all connected to each other and the natural world. Consequently, a sense of community and belonging abides and I feel safe, accepted and supported.

HOW I SEE THE REAL WORLD

I feel completely disconnected from the outside world and so I suffer from feelings of loss and abandonment. Even when I am at my most content, I still feel that there is something missing.

HOW I COPE WITH LIFE

The only way I can cope with life is to create my own fantasy world that loves and accepts me for who I am. It is the only place I feel complete.

KEY CHARACTERISTICS

I am

- Perceptive.
- Unique and different.
- Sensitive to what others are feeling.
- Empathetic with the suffering of others
- Investigative – a real Sherlock Holmes.
- Passionate.
- A true romantic.
- Full of deep emotions.
- A seeker of the truth.
- A soul searcher.

WHAT I HATE DEALING WITH

- Being or feeling ignored and abandoned.
- Feeling unimportant.
- Feeling defective.
- Boring people or situations.

HOW I THINK AND BEHAVE

- I romanticise the past.
- I long for something or somebody to rescue me and make it alright.

- I love connecting on a deep and sentimental level.

WHAT I DON'T SEE

- I fail to notice when others accept me for who I am.
- I try to avoid the ordinary in day-to-day living.

HOW I COMMUNICATE

- I am really energetic when expressing my feelings.
- I love to explore the possibilities.
- I focus on my sensations when I am talking to another.
- I am passionate in my communication.
- I analyse others' responses.

HOW I RESPOND TO EXAM STRESS

I become really very frightened because I fear that I won't live up to my ideals. Consequently, I become over-dramatic and almost hysterical, as the exams get closer. I will find lots of reasons for why I will fail and therefore, I prepare everyone for my mythical failure.

Also, my ability to listen to reason rapidly disappears because I've convinced myself that it is hopeless as I am completely flawed and defective (unlike all of my friends because they are so fantastic and they are everything I am not). Furthermore, I absolutely hate it when others boast about how well they think they are going to do.

However, what scares me the most is that by failing these exams, everyone will see that I am completely ordinary and not unique.

THE TOOLS I CAN USE TO DEAL WITH EXAM STRESS

- Stop focusing on what's missing and focus on what I do have.
- Keep a check on my emotions and stay focused on what I'm doing.

- Avoid negative people, who make me focus on what's wrong.
- Avoid competitive people, who make me feel paranoid; e.g. as if I'm not doing enough studying.
- Don't be pulled into the hysterical reactions exams can cause.
- Stay connected with my romantic ideals.
- During my study breaks, escape with a romantic book, film or music.
- Spend some time with an empathetic friend.
- Have a study buddy, who I can deeply connect with and feel supported by.
- Study how a wolf connects with its clan for support during difficult times.
- At the end of a very hard day, have a relaxing, soothing bath in soft light with my favourite scents and smells.

STUDY TIPS

- Create an exam study schedule.
- Each day, make a priority list with the most important at the top of the list.
- Use of highlighter pens and post-it-notes work really well, so make detailed notes on post-it-notes and place them on a wall in my room, or around the house.
- Play soothing, background music, which will help me to distress and keep me focused.
- Notice which subjects/topics I avoid, as this is an indication of my fear of them.
- Avoid emotional films and don't get drawn into any family or friendship group dramas.

- Find a creative outlet for all my fears and frustrations; e.g. doodling, diary writing, painting.
- Remind myself of the subjects I am good at.
- Plan ahead by being prepared in advance for each exam – not cramming the night before.

LEARNING STYLES

I am an effective learner when

- I can personally connect with the subject matter.
- I take responsibility for motivating myself to study.
- I have a supportive teacher who believes in me.
- I am able to make my work unique.
- I am given a chance to creatively express myself in the subject.
- I'm not being compared to others.
- I am included and my efforts are recognised.
- I'm given the opportunity and time to produce exceptional pieces of work.

GETTING SUPPORT FROM OTHERS

What would you say to your parents, carers and teachers who want to support you?

- Please, please do not put pressure on me or allow anyone else to pressurize me.
- It is really important for you to allow me to talk about how I am feeling emotionally because it helps me to release them.
- At least once a day, you have to remind me of all the things I have done well because it is so easy for me to forget and just focus on everything I've done badly instead.

- During stressful times, I really do need your support and attention to make me feel safe.
- I really appreciate it if you would help me question my own pessimistic and hopeless thoughts about life.
- I really need to believe that you have genuinely listened to me, so please can you demonstrate that in your communication.
- Please do not compare me to other students or siblings (or tell me what I should be achieving, especially if I'm not). It is the fastest way to encourage me to self-punish.
- I know I can be a little dramatic and I'd appreciate it if you can let me know when I become overly hysterical. Time out to calm down will stop me losing control.

AFFIRMATIONS TO HELP YOU STAY ON TRACK

My feelings are only part of me and don't control me.

I am grateful for my life, my friends and myself.

NB. For more affirmations, see details about the *Laid Back Guide Affirmation Cards* in the Appendices.

REMEMBER -

The Wolf guides you to connect with your wild side and discover your own hidden powers and gifts. The Wolf carries the gift of perseverance and encourages you to move through obstacles by finding creative ways around them.

By connecting with your intuition, you know the natural order of life and what is likely to happen next; therefore, trust your gut instinct. The Wolf reminds you that you have the ability to find solutions even in the darkest moments. You are a valued and respected clan member and the skills and resources you bring to the pack are crucial to its survival and success.

‘Ability is what you’re CAPABLE of doing. Motivation determines what you do.

Attitude determines how well you do it.’

Lou Holts

CHAPTER 5

THE TIGER

MY IDEAL WORLD

The world is an abundant and prosperous place with enough of everything for everyone. Everyone is treated fairly and has the chance to shine.

HOW I SEE THE REAL WORLD

The real world is a very tough and empty place, which drains people of their energy and resources.

HOW I COPE WITH LIFE

I'm really good at shutting out the outside world to protect myself.

Actually, I'm quite self-sufficient and very private; basically, I don't really need anyone or anything. This is how I manage to survive in this harsh, unforgiving world.

KEY CHARACTERISTICS

I am

- Studious.
- Very calm, cool and collected.
- Honourable and respectful.
- Considerate.
- Secretive.
- Dependable and responsible.
- Simplicity, like the simple things in life.
- Self-sufficient.
- Observer of life.

WHAT I HATE DEALING WITH

- Any intense feelings, including my own.
- My own fear.
- Invasive people, or environments that take my energy.
- My thoughts about being incompetent.
- Lack of energy because I can't cope with life.

HOW I THINK AND BEHAVE

- I file pieces of my life into different compartments.
- I live mainly in my head.
- I adore facts and analysis.
- I avoid demands and people who meddle in my life.

WHAT I DON'T SEE

- The opportunities and richness that life has to offer.
- That people are only too happy to support me.
- That I need to give more readily to myself.

HOW I COMMUNICATE

- Analytically.
- Calmly and clearly.
- Accurate with the detail.
- Distant.

HOW I RESPOND TO EXAM STRESS

I find exams to be inconvenient because I don't like my knowledge being questioned. This is really because I have a huge fear of being wrong as it makes me feel inadequate. I'm also really drained by exams because I don't have the time to relax and recharge.

The other thing that takes a lot of my energy is all that studying - and it's even worse when I get interrupted by everyone else in the household. There never seems to be enough time to do it all and I end up chasing my tail.

Furthermore, I get so worried about not having enough knowledge before sitting the exam, so it really irritates me when other people get hysterical about exams because it makes me even more anxious. I just can't deal with all that emotion!

THE TOOLS I CAN USE TO DEAL WITH EXAM STRESS

- Take some time out for myself to recharge my batteries.
- Go for a walk on my own and focus on what I see.

- Indulge myself by spending time on my own doing my favourite hobby or pastime.
- Go to the library or somewhere quiet to do my studying.
- Be aware of my body and eat healthily.
- Remember to give myself regular breaks, if necessary, put a timer on my watch.
- Accept my knowledge is enough and don't overdo it.
- Make sure I express my wants and needs to my family, friends and teachers.
- Avoid the demands of others.
- Be confident in my knowledge and understanding.
- Become more organised with my study notes and resources.
- Accept my feelings of anxiety and fear in this situation.

STUDY TIPS

- It's really important for me to make an exam study schedule, so I don't become overwhelmed by a lack of time.
- I really need to organise my notes into coloured and labelled files, so it is easy for me to find them.
- It's best if I start with a subject/topic I hate first because I will be tempted to put it off.
- I need to review exam questions so I only study what is needed, versus searching for everything on the subject.
- I could be part of a study group, so I can share my knowledge on a subject. This will boost my confidence, as I'll recognise how much I really know.
- I might have all the answers and there may be nothing to be frightened about.

- Mind maps and spider diagrams are an excellent study tool for me.
- I must limit my study time, so I can maintain my energy levels.
- I need to put some headphones on and listen to, 'white noise' music, so other people don't disturb me.

LEARNING STYLES

I am an effective learner when

- I'm using my observation skills; e.g. listening to lectures, YouTube, etc.
- I am given time to gather lots of knowledge before presenting it.
- I am given lots of information about a subject/topic.
- I really enjoy investigating and experimenting with different perspectives and viewpoints.
- I work much better when I am left alone to do what I need to do.
- I much prefer learning a lot about a topic versus a little about a lot of topics.
- I'm given the opportunity to discuss topics I have a lot of knowledge about.
- I'm given thinking time because I need time to process all the potential solutions.

GETTING SUPPORT FROM OTHERS

What would you like to say to your parents, carers and teachers who want to support you?

- Please don't interfere with my choices because it makes me feel incapable and inadequate.
- I like to be independent and hate to share my feelings. Please be

aware of that because I don't know how to express myself emotionally (actually it really frightens me).

- Please help me to get in touch with my fearful feelings about exams by being a very, very good listener.
- Don't try to make me do things that you think I'd like to do.
- I feel really awkward and 'geeky' in the outside world and often feel lonely in a crowd because I think that there is something wrong with me.
- Please confirm to me that I'm an excellent observer and that my observations are very valuable, like Watson does to Sherlock Holmes.
- Encourage me to be part of the picture in school/university by helping me to belong.
- Encourage me to share my knowledge on topics of interest with like-minded people and I will then feel validated and gain more confidence.

AFFIRMATIONS TO HELP YOU STAY ON TRACK

My life is full of meaning and I am competent and appreciated.

I accept others and include them in my life and I am open to their ideas.

NB. For more affirmations, see details about the *Laid Back Guide Affirmation Cards* in the Appendices.

REMEMBER -

The Tiger is here to guide you to connect with the knowledge you already have. You are also encouraged to recognise your innate strength and undaunting courage in the darkness of the unknown. By maintaining your focus and belief in yourself and your environment, you can develop a bold ferocity to hunt down and capture your heartfelt desires.

You are invited to meditate on the Tiger's courage and endurance to help you unlock that same power within yourself. Use the rhythms and motions of the environment to your advantage like the Tiger does and know that you belong. When you need to recharge your batteries, follow the Tiger to its secret lair, so you can let your visions unfold.

'Stop worrying about the potholes in the road and celebrate the journey.'

Barbara Hoffman

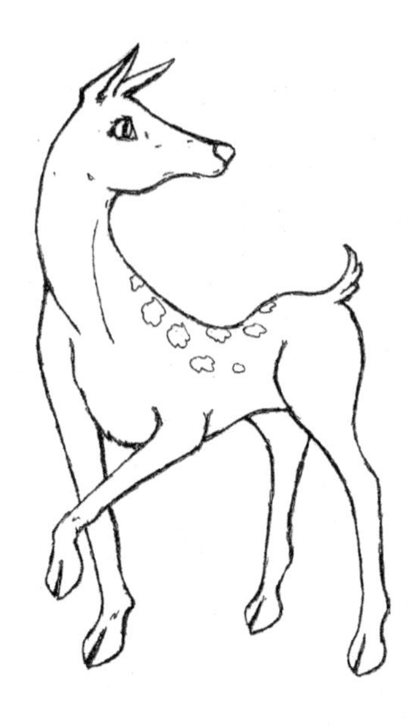

CHAPTER 6

THE DEER

MY IDEAL WORLD

I believe that the world is a safe place where everyone is trustworthy. I also rely on my own inner intuition to guide me in my decisions.

HOW I SEE THE REAL WORLD

The world is a dangerous place where I don't feel safe because I fear that something bad is bound to happen. How can I possibly trust others, as well as myself, in a world like this?

HOW I COPE WITH LIFE

I am really very complex because I am so aware of the danger all around me. Consequently, I might be the type who goes along with the rest of the crowd, or I might doubt and question everything and everyone, eventually rebelling because of it. So, I'm a creature of extremes: either obeying authority, or rebelling against authority.

KEY CHARACTERISTICS

I am

- Reliable.
- Intuitive.
- Faithful.
- Considerate.
- Inquisitive.
- Determined.
- Responsible.
- Conscientious.
- Wry and have a dry sense of humour.
- Sympathetic.
- Full of self-doubt.

WHAT I HATE DEALING WITH

- Becoming a victim.
- Conflict.
- Abandonment.
- Change and not being in control of my life.
- Confusion and not knowing what to do.

HOW I THINK AND BEHAVE

- I always focus on what is wrong.

- I identify all the possible dangers.
- I look for inconsistency, especially in people, and focus on their actions rather than what they say.

WHAT I DON'T SEE

- That I make mountains out of molehills.
- That I tend to focus only on the negative.

HOW I COMMUNICATE

- I will go into depth and detail.
- I speak at two speeds: either very quickly, or very thoughtfully.
- I ask lots of questions, especially 'what if' questions.
- I focus on the facts and figures.

HOW I RESPOND TO EXAM STRESS

I become really anxious and indecisive like, 'Have I got all my notes?' 'Have I got my exam schedule?' 'What do I study first?' Basically, I become so worried and worked up that my anxiety reaches catastrophic levels.

I also become very stubborn and have to do things my way. Then I think I've done it wrong and worry even more.

At this stage, I've lost all faith in myself and doubt my ability to do anything correctly and doubt everybody and everything else. However, the truth is I'm so scared because I feel I can't trust anyone and I believe the world is a very scary and horrible place.

THE TOOLS I CAN USE TO DEAL WITH EXAM STRESS

- Accept that I'm scared and it's ok for me to be scared.
- Meditation will help me to ground myself back to reality.

- Lots of positive praise from teachers, parents and my friends will help me to feel that I'm on the right track.
- Know that it is normal to feel a little stressed.
- Ask my parents or carers to help me set guidelines for having a healthy routine during exams.
- Recognise that I matter and that I am safe. Remind myself that it's just an exam.
- Think of three things I can do to change my negative thoughts to positive ones.
- Be open to expert advice, even if it might differ from my own.
- Deal with one issue at a time. Don't let myself become overwhelmed by thinking about all the possible issues.
- Select a positive role model from films, or books whose strengths I admire and use them in this situation.
- What 10 positive qualities did I have as a young, curious child? Could I redevelop them? This could help me find the balance and harmony I want.
- Spend time with a positive group of friends during exams versus friends who will make me worry even more.
- Play analytical structured games as a form of release e.g. chess, computer role playing games or strategy games.
- Use my dry sense of humour and see the funny side to exams.
- Stop doubting myself and remember that I am very gifted and capable.

STUDY TIPS

- Create an exam study schedule.
- Buy a study guide for each subject.

- Ask my teachers about how the exam is structured and learn the structure.
- Learn how to plan effectively because it will help me in the exam.
- Gather and file my notes into some sort of order again.
- Make sure I know what to do for each question by reading it very carefully.
- Make sure my class notes are accurate, up-to-date and detailed.
- Note that I learn best by observation. I'm a visual learner, so perhaps watch how my teacher structures answers to exam practice questions and ask for a copy.
- Don't over-analyse my thoughts or my written responses because it will paralyse me.

LEARNING STYLES

I am an effective learner when

- I stop blaming others for my own fear.
- I am open to expert advice.
- I trust my inner gut feeling.
- I build positive relationships with teachers.
- I stay in a safe, anxiety-free environment e.g. a library.
- I recognize my capacity for hard work and commitment.
- I am trusted to be an effective learner.
- I'm given the opportunity to ask the teacher questions.
- I am given the opportunity to share my anxiety before work starts.

GETTING SUPPORT FROM OTHERS

What would you say to your parents, carers and teachers who want to support you?

- Please, please take the time to listen to me (and my views) because I feel so uncomfortable and incapable of communicating them clearly, that sometimes I don't share them at all. Instead, I'll keep them to myself and just worry.
- I really need you to be honest with me and reassure me about my unnecessary fears. I know I tend to get quite angry and aggressive when I'm scared, especially when I'm lost as to what to do. However, this is the time when I need you to be calm and bear with my overreaction.
- Please understand how overwhelmed I am by worry and change. I really don't feel safe in the world and too much change too quickly can send me over the edge.
- Encouraging me to feel physically confident and ok in myself will really help me to feel safe and also feel as if I can do things well. So whether it's riding a bike, or clearing out a cupboard, your positive praise is vital in supporting me in feeling positive about my abilities as well as myself.
- The best way to get me out of my dark space is to have a laugh and a joke with me.
- Please be the best mentor you can be and someone I feel safe in confiding in.

AFFIRMATIONS TO HELP YOU STAY ON TRACK

I trust myself and everyone I meet.

I now act with strength and confidence in all areas in my life.

NB. For more affirmations, see details about the *Laid Back Guide Affirmation Cards* in the Appendices.

REMEMBER -

The Deer invites you to accept your positive, inner guidance and authority. It reminds you that you are a leader who does know where you are going and also has the ability to navigate life by tapping into your inner resources. The Deer is highly sensitive and intuitive, as are you. You can pick up on the thoughts and feelings of others, which is why your hypervigilance is a gift to be celebrated.

The Deer is able to change direction and invites you to do the same without fearing the unknown. Just remember to balance your instinct for going in a certain direction, with thoughtful consideration of how you are going to get there. This is what will keep you completely centred like the Deer is within its environment.

Finally, like the Deer, being outside is very good for you as it recharges and regenerates you. It is important for you to be part of a similar herd of people because it makes you feel safe.

'The moment you take responsibility for everything in your life is the moment you can change anything in your life'.

Hal Elrod.

CHAPTER 7

THE OTTER

MY IDEAL WORLD

I am free to explore all opportunities that are available to me. In this world, I am focused and committed because I am not restricted or constrained by anyone or anything.

HOW I SEE THE REAL WORLD

The world can be a confining place because I am constantly stopped from doing the things that I really want to do. Consequently, I feel trapped and it causes me to experience painful thoughts and feelings, which is something I really don't like feeling.

HOW I COPE WITH LIFE

I've learnt to focus my attention on feeling positive emotions only, whilst repressing any negative ones. I do this by deliberately seeking out exciting opportunities and also making sure that I don't stand still long enough to feel anything negative.

KEY CHARACTERISTICS

I am

- Fun.
- Imaginative.
- Very sociable.
- Helpful.
- Spontaneous.
- Free-spirited.
- Generous.
- Excitable.

WHAT I HATE DEALING WITH

- Feeling bored.
- Negative emotions.
- Being trapped and constrained.
- People who are depressed and depressing situations.

HOW I THINK AND BEHAVE

- I am enthusiastic and optimistic: always looking at the bright and fun side of life.
- I love being around others, and am considered the life and soul of the party.

- I really enjoy doing adventurous things.
- I love being a trendsetter because it always gets me noticed.
- I always justify my behaviour, especially when I'm in a tight corner.

WHAT I DON'T SEE

- I don't see or acknowledge the negative aspects of life.
- I refuse to see any restrictions or boundaries to my desires.

HOW I COMMUNICATE

- I speak very quickly.
- I change topics often.
- I'm very enthusiastic.
- I like to focus the conversation on myself.

HOW I RESPOND TO EXAM STRESS

I find exams so restrictive and boring, which causes me to feel huge levels of stress. It is especially stressful because I begin to experience those horrible, negative feelings, which I hate experiencing and want to run away from. I'd much rather *do* something fun, like go shopping, or play on the latest computer game.

Also, I hate that these exams interrupt my social life. Instead, I feel trapped, helpless and frustrated because I have been limited and restricted by the exam process. Consequently, I am more likely to act out, throw a tantrum and certainly not study properly. Anyway, I'm pretty bright and great at waffling. And so what if I fail? Not that I will. There's always tomorrow: isn't there?

THE TOOLS I CAN USE TO DEAL WITH EXAM STRESS

- Unusual locations to study in.
- Schedule some adventurous activities during exam time: e.g. horse riding, bike riding etc.
- Recognise that the exam period is only for a short time.
- Be self-disciplined and tick off the days during the exam period.
- Organise an end of exam celebration party.
- List all the positive outcomes of taking the exams.
- Don't use alcohol, drugs or any other substances to escape.
- Acknowledge my painful feelings and write them on a piece of paper, then burn it.
- Think of three things I could do to improve and transform my feelings of boredom.
- Focus on the qualifications I can receive.
- Visualise myself opening my results on results day.
- Recognise my resistance towards taking exams.
- Acknowledge my fear and use the energy toward exam preparation.
- When I'm feeling frustrated, bounce a basketball or punch a punch-bag.

STUDY TIPS

- Create my own unique, computerised exam study schedule.
- Turn off my phone and avoid any distractions in the time I choose to study.
- Listen to music whilst studying, as it will keep me focused.
- Set an alarm for 40 minutes study time, and then take a short break.

- Study responsibly with others by setting clear ground rules.
- Get my friends to test me on my subject/topic by having a group quiz.
- Brainstorm answers to exam questions with my study group.
- Get help from a friend on subjects I struggle with.
- Check in with my tutor or teacher on a regular basis to monitor how I am doing.

LEARNING STYLES

I am an effective learner when

- Learning is fun and engaging.
- The teacher is enthusiastic and spontaneous.
- The task can be broken down into a variety of activities.
- There are lively debates and discussions around topics.
- When I can brainstorm ideas in a group.
- I learn very quickly and can relate my learning to the real world.
- I am able to hypothesise with ideas and theories.
- I have to fill in the gaps because it encourages me to use my inner problem-solving talents.

GETTING SUPPORT FROM OTHERS

What would you say to your parents, carers and teachers who want to support you?

- I might appear to be really confident and seem to know what I'm doing, but really, I'm very hurt and anxious. So, I really value the opportunity to share how I'm really feeling, without being judged.
- Please help me to overcome my resistance to exams by helping me to understand and see the bigger picture.

- You can help me to take responsibility by calmly talking through the consequences of my choices and actions, especially the impulsive ones. This way, I can learn to think before I act.
- If you ground me or restrict me from seeing my friends, I will lie or do something dangerous to see them. This is because having contact with my friends is the one thing that helps me to de-stress.
- Joking around with me and using humour, especial within the home, is a great motivator.
- I really could do with a trustworthy mentor who will guide me through the difficult day-to-day events that I might not wish to look at or even acknowledge.
- I do need guidance on how much freedom is healthy for me because I often do not know how to place limits on what I can or cannot handle.
- Please encourage me to be myself versus a caricature of someone I admire.

AFFIRMATIONS TO HELP YOU STAY ON TRACK

I am peaceful when I stop and connect with things around me.

I listen quietly to what others share with me as I value their friendship.

NB. For more affirmations, see details about the *Laid Back Guide Affirmation Cards* in the Appendices.

REMEMBER -

The Otter is a light-hearted, sociable character, who exudes warmth and humour whilst remaining very focused and determined on what needs to be done. The Otter has learnt the art of finding enjoyment and adventure in all that it does by exploring the possibilities available to it.

It encourages you to recognise the power of freedom that does come from commitment and invites you to swim with it in the rivers of life. Sometimes those rivers will be playful, and at others will be raging. No matter which it is, the otter is confident in demonstrating its emotions; for instance, when catching a fish, it expresses its joy, and when there is danger present, it expresses its fear and anxiety.

Learn how the Otter uses its innate skills and emotions to lead a fulfilling, free and joyful existence, whilst also being responsible and able to accomplish its tasks.

'Assertiveness is your ability to act in harmony with your self-esteem, without hurting anyone.'

Anon

CHAPTER 8

THE BEAR

MY IDEAL WORLD

The world is full of honourable, truthful and vulnerable people who can safely express their feelings in the moment, without being criticized or ridiculed for having them.

HOW I SEE THE REAL WORLD

It is a hard, unjust corrupt world where the dominant few control the weak and gullible. It is a place where there is no equality and you become controlled, unless you resist it.

HOW I COPE WITH LIFE

I learned to toughen up and lock any weakness into a box. Also, I learned to become protective of the underdog, the helpless and myself by developing my authority and leadership qualities. This is how I have gained respect and recognition. I always trust my gut feelings, as they are always right.

KEY CHARACTERISTICS

I am

- Brave.
- Determined.
- Righteous.
- Assertive.
- Vigilant and always ready to spring into action.
- Confident.
- Passionate.
- Amiable.
- Selfless.
- Influential.

WHAT I HATE DEALING WITH

- Ambiguous people and situations.
- Being reliant and dependent on others.
- My own inner weaknesses because they make me feel vulnerable.
- Losing the respect of others, especially my peers.

HOW I THINK AND BEHAVE

- I am a natural leader and will take charge at every opportunity.

- I am not afraid to take the necessary action to get where I want to go.
- I take great pleasure in protecting the weak and innocent.
- I earn respect by being powerful and fair.
- I really need to demonstrate control over my environment and myself.

WHAT I DON'T SEE

- How I can overpower others with my dominant and passionate energy.
- Other views of the world because *only* mine are correct.

HOW I COMMUNICATE

- I'm very blunt, honest and direct.
- I'm very enthusiastic and authoritative.
- I'm combative and antagonistic, especially when it comes to fairness.

HOW I RESPOND TO EXAM STRESS

I become really jittery around exam-time because I feel vulnerable and unsure. Also, I'm scared about losing the respect of my friends if I show it. Consequently, I can become really grumpy and uncooperative to hide my real feelings of insecurity.

Actually, I am scared of failure so I'll avoid it at all costs, even if it means that I get into trouble at school. In fact, I feel really isolated because I've got no one I can share my real feelings with. I might even develop a phobia of exams and fall into a depressive state.

So, don't be surprised if I become more resistant in school and in lessons as we get closer to the exam. I'll even pretend I don't care by doing very little in class. It doesn't matter if you give me a detention because I'll use my false bravado to rebel against your control.

THE TOOLS I CAN USE TO DEAL WITH EXAM STRESS

- Physical activity to release all that pent up energy.
- Consider a time-out card to control my pent up frustrations.
- Recognise the benefits of additional support and welcome it.
- Seek out an adult mentor I can trust to share my real feelings (e.g. teacher, grandparent, parent, carer).
- Stop and think before taking any impulsive action.
- Go and find a calm and quiet place where I can release the tension.
- Learn to compromise.
- Make sure I get plenty of rest versus continuing to push myself.
- Recognise and own my vulnerable feelings.
- Value my gentleness and my sensitivity because I really can be a cuddly bear.
- Don't turn to alcohol, drugs or smoking to escape my real feelings.
- Be open to different ways of approaching exams and give them a try for at least a week.
- Speak to my teachers about any topics I am struggling with.
- Become an exam buddy for someone who might be struggling in my favourite topic.

STUDY TIPS

- Create my own exam study schedule to suit me.
- Join in classroom discussion and debates to learn more about my subjects.
- Reinforce my learning by introducing practical elements to my studying (e.g. watch the movie of a novel).

- Use flash cards to jot down key facts and figures.
- Do practice tests and score myself.
- Create power points for my topics and look to share this with others.
- Make links between my subjects and the real world (e.g. banking and percentages.)
- Team up with people who would benefit from my knowledge.
- Attend any additional school study sessions or one-to-one sessions.

LEARNING STYLES

I am an effective learner when

- Learning is interactive and physical.
- I respect the teacher and the rules.
- We get straight to the point versus deviate.
- There is a set routine within the lesson.
- Tasks are set and I'm left to get on with it.
- Most of my learning is done at school.
- There is an opportunity to debate and discuss topics.
- I can relate what I am learning to my career choice.

GETTING SUPPORT FROM OTHERS

What would you say to your parents, carers and teachers who want to support you?

- I might come across as brash and arrogant; however, I'd like you to help me to reveal my sensitive side by being considerate of my feelings.
- Be open and honest when you are giving me feedback because I'll

know if you are deceiving me; especially if you try to give me false hope.

- Please give me the opportunity to express my own opinions and I will be open to hearing yours too.
- Definitely never, ever talk down to me or call me stupid because I will lose my temper.
- If I'm about to lose my temper, please give me the respect and opportunity to have some time out and calm down.
- Being in a calm, grounded environment helps me to stay calm.
- Don't allow me to get bored because boredom leads to trouble for me. Therefore, give me something productive to do, or make me responsible for something.
- Fairness is a huge issue for me and I'd welcome the opportunity to express my opinion on it, especially when I feel I am not being treated fairly.

AFFIRMATIONS TO HELP YOU STAY ON TRACK

It is safe for me to release control over: self, others and my environment.

It is safe for me to show people my caring side.

NB. For more affirmations, see details about the *Laid Back Guide Affirmation Cards* in the Appendices.

REMEMBER -

The Bear invites you to embrace your natural leadership qualities and strong presence. However, the Bear also asks you to accept your powerful, protective and healing qualities to support, as well as protect those more vulnerable than yourself. The Bears' perseverance means that they have the ability to achieve their goals, and overcome obstacles in their path, as do you.

Also, the Bears' innate wisdom means they recognise the need to take time out by themselves where they can reconnect and gain a new perspective on: themselves, others and situations. Once they have digested these new ideas and emerged from their cave, their new perspective and mature attitude brings them the respect and recognition they deserve.

Watch how the Bear operates in the natural world and consider how the bear uses their gut instinct to guide them towards their dreams, goals and ideal outcomes.

‘Focus on one thing, make it your priority and stick with it, no matter what.’

Tyler Perry

CHAPTER 9

THE ORANGUTAN

MY IDEAL WORLD

Everyone is supportive, caring and understanding. They are all connected with each other and with their environment, and live in a caring supportive, community.

HOW I SEE THE REAL WORLD

The world makes people's individual presence unimportant, which requires them to conform to society's standards in order to be accepted, instead of being unconditionally accepted for who they really are.

HOW I COPE WITH LIFE

I've learned to overly cooperate with others, because it's easier than putting my wants and needs first. Also, I make the best of situations, instead of pursuing or fighting for what I really want. Other people's wants and needs are more important than my own.

KEY CHARACTERISTICS

I am

- Very caring and approachable.
- Overly pleasing to others.
- Adaptable to what others want of me.
- Totally in tune with others.
- Considerate and nurturing.
- Highly responsible.
- Reliable.
- Flexible.

WHAT I HATE DEALING WITH

- Arguments and battles.
- Feeling troubled and hopeless.
- Feeling overwhelmed and put upon.
- Feeling neglected.

HOW I THINK AND BEHAVE

- I am constantly thinking about other people's wants, needs and desires.
- I love to connect with nature and the natural world.
- I really love rescuing people and animals in distress.

- I've learned how to blend into my environment and become part of the furniture.
- I like to solve conflicts quickly because I dislike the disharmony and any changes to my life.

WHAT I DON'T SEE

- The need for me to develop my individuality.
- My need to be assertive.

HOW I COMMUNICATE

- Diplomatic and careful with the language I use.
- Cooperative and very good listening skills because of my empathy.
- I over-explain my feelings and my thoughts to merge with another.
- Serene and peaceful tone.

HOW I RESPOND TO EXAM STRESS

Exams interrupt my peaceful world because they bring huge change and have expectations attached to them. I really, really struggle in motivating myself to participate in the preparation for the exams. I have no idea of how to make time for studying because, usually, I'm too busy looking after everyone else.

Consequently, I become really overwhelmed because my day-to-day life is going to have to dramatically change to cater for the exams. How can I possibly find the time to study everything for every subject in the time I've been allocated? I feel so pressured.

With everybody making demands on my time and energy, I begin to shut down and shut myself away because it seems as if no one else cares for me; all they want is for me to be there for them.

THE TOOLS I CAN USE TO DEAL WITH EXAM STRESS

- Create a complete, phone-free chill-out zone, where I can just lay back, listen to relaxing music and drift away.
- 15-minute meditation each day.
- Have a motivational quote wall.
- Hatha yoga before studying will help ground me.
- Study with friends, but make sure I'm not doing all the work.
- Identify how I waste time avoiding change and exam preparation.
- Learn to have a future focus to work towards.
- Learn to put boundaries in place with friends and family.
- Limit my television, game playing and social media time to an hour a day.
- Make sure I get a supportive hug from somebody I trust.
- Make *me* important, by asking for what I want and need – try asking for this *at least* once a day.
- Each day make a list of priorities then tick it off once I've completed it.
- Make sure I'm ok, before I run around caring for the neighbourhood.
- Find an assertive and responsible study buddy, who will help keep me grounded and on track.

STUDY TIPS

- Create a mind map exam study schedule.
- For each study session, set my alarm for when I should start and when the session will end.
- Make sure that I'm grounded and focused by turning off my cell phone and all other technologies, so that I am not distracted.

- Create a calm atmosphere or go to the local library.
- Make sure I have had something healthy to eat and drink.
- Decide which topics/subjects I need to study first by cross-checking it with my exam schedule.
- Go through past papers and highlight questions I need to study for.
- Stand in the middle of the room and have a shake break. This helps to reenergise and refocus me.
- Make sure there is plenty of ventilation in my study room.
- Put Post-it-notes on the wall in my room and on my work to really help motivate me.
- Use of highlighters are a great way for me to remember important key facts and figures.

LEARNING STYLES

I am an effective learner when

- I am able to explore the subject in depth.
- I am in a calm environment.
- I can recap new learning repeatedly until I am familiar with it.
- I am able to be creative with what I am learning.
- I learn in a quiet group where there is little conflict.
- Clear, focused written and verbal feedback from the teacher.
- When there is a routine in place.
- I prevent myself from drifting off into my daydreams.

GETTING SUPPORT FROM OTHERS

What would you say to your parents, carers and teachers who want to support you?

- Although I'm usually amiable and diplomatic, I am very easily hurt (although I may not show it), so please can you check out that I'm ok on a regular basis.
- I can become really angry, but dismiss it, even though it matters. Please support me by helping me to connect with my anger and show me ways to release it (like writing my thoughts down e.g. a letter that's not going to be posted).
- I repress my real needs by zoning out and refocusing my attention on either unhealthy food, or excessive TV or social media stuff.
- Help me reconnect by supporting me in setting up my priorities.
- Please help me to feel safe around change and studying by breaking big tasks down into little ones.
- Please help me to remember to focus on *me* because my presence counts to myself, as well as to others.
- Encourage me to be assertive and confident in expressing my opinions.
- Help me to establish healthy boundaries that support my progress, and celebrate when I remember to apply them to real life situations.

AFFIRMATIONS TO HELP YOU STAY ON TRACK

My presence counts to others and myself.

I am really supportive and strong during difficult times.

NB. For more affirmations, see details about the *Laid Back Guide Affirmation Cards* in the Appendices.

REMEMBER -

The Orangutan invites you to go within and seek out your natural gifts that will help you to deal with everyday problems. Although hugely compassionate toward others, the Orangutan encourages you to demonstrate the same compassion and care to yourself.

You need to become more expressive with your communication by using your body language effectively to emphasise your meaning. You are also invited to be aware of the body language in others, as it can highlight what they are not saying to you.

The Orangutan teaches you about your own resourcefulness and appreciating the impact of the simple things in life that are readily available to you. The Orangutan connects with its environment and gains strength from the natural surroundings. It appreciates the need for solitude to recharge its batteries and recognises the energy it gains.

CHAPTER 10

GREMLINS WITHIN

The partial Oxford (2015) definition of a gremlin is, 'An imaginary mischievous sprite...'. However, they are much more than that. They are also your critical voice - you know the one that lives inside your head and is always criticizing you and putting you down. These gremlins are definitely mischief- makers.

In this chapter, we have some information to share with you about your gremlins. But first, here is a gremlin story you might be familiar with.

A GREMLIN STORY

Here is the story of a baby girl who attracted a gremlin called, '*Your Presence Does Not Matter.*'

When she was born, her parents were not keen on having children. Children were noisy, demanding and messy, with toys everywhere. Her parents were determined that their baby girl was going to learn to adapt to their wishes by being quiet, not make a mess or be noisy, like other children. In fact, she was going to learn not to make any demands at all.

She spent her childhood outside, wandering alone and quiet in the fields by her home. You see, her mother wanted her out from under her feet most of the time. Her gremlin kept telling her that she must not upset her mummy because her mummy would not love, or even like her. Certainly not as much as her mother's favourite and special poodle, who could do nothing wrong in her mother's eyes.

How her gremlin made her hate that dog.

By the time she had became a preteen, oh boy, her gremlin had grown bigger and stronger too. He was constantly telling her how unattractive, useless and clumsy she was. Her mother would help the gremlin too by agreeing wholeheartedly with him.

'For goodness sake, stand up straight! Be quiet, and turn that music off! Can't you find something useful to do?'

Her gremlin was having so much trickster fun. Furthermore, because the teenager believed him about her presence not mattering to her parents, she spent hour upon hour in her bedroom, lying on her bed feeling unwanted and unloved. She felt so dejected that she spent her time dreaming of her favourite singer and the kind of life she would be living if only her presence mattered.

However, she didn't give in – no way! Instead, she decided to rebel and make a stand. Her belief that things had got to change was just too strong. So, she decided to go and buy some clothes that her mother and father would hate.

She thought, 'Yes, this will make the difference. People have to notice me now!'

However, while putting on her leather jacket, black mini skirt and tight top, her gremlin decided to strike.

'Bet you won't even get past the front door. You look a mess!' he sneered.

She desperately tried to ignore the gremlin and continued on her mission. But when she bravely went downstairs, she was severely told off and sent to her room to take off her 'trashy' clothes and wash her face clean of all 'that make-up muck'.

Yes, she certainly got attention, but her presence mattered even less now and her feelings of unworthiness grew ten times worse.

MEET THE REAL GREMLIN

Our inner gremlins sometimes like to trick us into thinking about out-dated beliefs that they want us to believe about ourselves including false thoughts and feelings about our lives, and how we should act and behave. They might like to whisper false ideas. For example:

- We may feel that we have no self-worth.
- We may feel that we could fail.
- We may think that we might not matter.

No matter what the beliefs or ideas are, our gremlins might be very persistent and might be so convincing that we believe them.

Honestly, we do!

These little tricksters love to lurk in the shadowy parts of our mind and soul. You see, they don't like us having happy, comforting, helpful thoughts about ourselves.

THEIR MISSION

Our gremlin's real mission is to steer us away from our true selves – sometimes known as our higher selves – that part of us that wants to grow, understand, have fun and enjoy life. Even when we are having fun, our gremlin might whisper doubts in our mind.

Unfortunately, they can give us very little breathing space and can be evasive. However, if you listen hard enough, you might begin to hear them. We hope you will try because it is only by hearing them that you have the chance of befriending them.

Take a moment now and just start to hear their voice. What's it sound like?

Next, imagine you are doing something that you really enjoy right now, something you rarely allow yourself to do. What did you just hear inside your head? What did you sense or feel? If it was negative, it is likely to be your gremlin's voice tricking you into not succeeding in the way you could; thereby, encouraging you to resist and stopping you from having the understanding of others, or their love and approval.

Ok, we hear you say, 'Don't be daft! I have the life and love I want.'

And you might well have. However, is there - by any chance- a little voice trying to make you doubt that? Well if there is, even a very tiny little voice inside you, then that might be your gremlin. They are trying hard to get you to react to them and sabotage your good self in some way. Maybe, they are encouraging you to think or say hurtful things about your best friend. Or, they may make you act in a negative way. This is because they want you to. The thing is, your mischievous, hurtful, gremlin within loves getting you into a cycle of negative thought patterns and beliefs by *gremlinizing* you. It's how it thrives and survives.

GREMLIN IN ACTION

Now, let us continue exploring the gremlin in action. Imagine the little girl in the gremlin story is now 16 and the gremlin has an even stronger hold on her than ever before. She is going to a party and is making a lot of effort to look good. She has spent some time getting ready, looking in the mirror. While she is looking in the mirror, she hears the gremlin's voice sneakily saying,

'Don't know why you're bothering. Nobody's interested in you. Have you had a real good look recently? Who on earth is going to be interested in your rat-tail hair, ugly face and, Oh my goodness! Have you looked at your body recently?'

This is our little trickster at work again because he is feeding off of her lack of self-worth.

However, sometimes we don't really pay attention to our gremlin. Instead, we distract ourselves from our little trickster voice; perhaps for some of us, we don't even hear it. It's a bit like a familiar mumble in the background. But that doesn't mean it's harmless. In fact, it's far from harmless because it is busy working in our unconscious by directing and controlling us without us even realising it. Your gremlin is sowing trickster seeds to make you believe it. And before you know it, wham! It has done it again. You see, what you think is what you get. So, if we go back to our poor soul who is busy dressing up and looking terrific; what might she experience or get this evening at the party?

Can you possibly guess?

Yes, you've guessed it. Having overcome and dismissed her little trickster, she's on her way to the party feeling quite sad and criticized. Yes, when she gets to the party, she might be the lonely person in the corner where nobody will notice her and out pops her gremlin.

"Look at all these beautiful people, who are far better than you. Who's going to look at *you*? You're going to just sit here all on your own. (Hehe). Like I told you. I told you, you are trashy."

As a consequence, she becomes sadder and sadder; and thereby, completely believing that she doesn't matter, no matter how hard she tries. Yep, our friend might have been well and truly *gremlinized*, without actually knowing what has happened. Our friend may come home from the party feeling dejected and unloved again, probably thinking, 'Why? Why, does this keep happening to me?'

However, your story may be a different one. It may have an entirely different content. But, I bet that your gremlin may probably have had a go at *gremlinizing* you at some time. The point is that we all have our own gremlin that affects our lives in many different ways.

The funny thing is that our friends and family can often see our gremlins better than we can. They kind of know when you are being *gremlinized* and when your gremlin is steering you away from that peace inside yourself. But, they don't always know what to say or do to stop the process. That's because only you can deal with your inner gremlin and have a proper exchange with it. You see it actually wants you to notice its presence. But, it is not allowed to jump out of your shadow and present itself to you until you ask it to.

Ok. So you're now, hopefully, getting the idea of how your critical voice or gremlin works. Also, you know those resentments? Guess who said those first? Yes, that's right. It's our friend, the gremlin. And you know those scary thoughts or tactics that stop you from succeeding? Yes, those are down to your gremlin too. So, don't you owe it to yourself to let your gremlin have a break and sleep for a while, and have a go at being in charge without it?

BEFRIENDING YOUR GREMLIN

So, let's go back to our teenager from the disastrous party. Where is our teenager now? Is she now wearing an imaginary tee shirt for the whole world to see with the words, 'My presence will never matter. Ever?'

Unfortunately she is. She spends her days sulking in her bedroom, feeling very sorry for herself, continuing to dream of her Prince Charming and wondering if he'll ever come to rescue her from this prison of self-loathing.

You might also be wondering whether Prince Charming will come? He might, but I wonder how he will treat her when her inner gremlins have got such a hold? How do you imagine he would treat her? Go on, and take a guess.

Yes, you're right! He will make her like him. Then as soon as she is hooked on him, guess what? He might reinforce her beliefs about herself by making her feel like her presence does not matter by ignoring her in some way. Perhaps by flirting with her best friend? Or by saying they have finished? Or telling her about how unimportant she is in his life?

You might well have a similar story going on and on with you or your friend right now. Over the years, I am sure, that your gremlins have created a few painful, hurtful, toxic situations for you, too. You see, when you listen to your gremlin and believe what it tells you, you also end up attracting experiences that reinforce your gremlin's message.

However, you can fight back. Are you ready to make a stand against them?

Ok. So here's the secret to taking charge of your gremlin. You need to befriend it instead of allowing it to control you.

The key to befriending it is by discovering your gremlin's name. By naming your gremlin, you'll draw it from its hiding place. Even by asking, it's a sure way to get it out of that dark, trickster place. Your gremlin's name could be: *'You Will Never Succeed'*, *'Failure'*, *'You're a Loser'* or *'You Don't Matter'*. On the other hand, it could be something completely different.

Take a moment now to, mentally, look it straight in the eye and ask for its name. Once you have, your gremlin can't trick you anymore because you have gained power by discovering its name. Congratulations! You have now taken your first step toward gaining control over your inner-gremlin.

From this moment, you will always be able to hear your gremlin's name because it loves to criticize. Most of the negative words spoken to you by your gremlin will include its name, so you'll always be able to identify whether that inner voice is coming from your higher self, or whether it's the voice of your gremlin.

Now we've shared this secret, your gremlin will really dislike us; especially, for suggesting that you meet and greet it. You see, your gremlin now knows it will lose a lot of its power from this day onwards; particularly, if you say the opposite of its name. For example, the gremlin called, '*Your Presence Doesn't Matter'* loses its power if you keep saying:

'My presence counts,' over and over again, until you start to believe it.

Now come on! Don't take any notice of your gremlin saying, 'Don't believe anything they say. It's rubbish!'

I hope you've heard it say these words because it will have said that, or something similar.

MASTERING YOUR GREMLIN

Mastering your gremlin is no easy thing because it's requiring you to be aware of when your gremlin is beginning to manipulate you. To determine whether it is your gremlin, try the following:

First, ask yourself this question, 'Do I know whether what I am experiencing is true?' To discover the truth, separate what's real from the imagined.

Next, be aware of your gremlin's active name, e.g. '*Your Presence Doesn't Matter*', '*You're Worthless*' or '*Nobody Loves You.*'

Finally, take a moment to think about the animal clan guides, 'Do our animal friends suffer from gremlins?' Possibly not because they are born knowing their real selves and so they live their lives in the moment, uncontaminated by mind-confusing gremlins. Maybe, that is why it is useful to gain their aid and observe how your particular animal clan guide lives its life gremlin-free.

Now, let us connect with our animal clan guides' pure selves and see how we could live our lives differently; less *gremlinized* and more in touch with our higher and pure self:

- The swan tells you to believe that you are good enough.
- The dog tells you how loved and wanted you are.
- The lion tells you how valuable and worthwhile you are.
- The wolf tells you how unique and extraordinary just being you is.
- The tiger tells you how useful and capable you are.
- The deer tells you to trust your gut instincts.
- The otter tells you how you can be taken care of.
- The bear tells you how you are protected.
- The orangutan tells you how much your voice and opinions count.

So now, you should move to your animal clan guides' magical space and start noticing, accepting and experiencing their energy within you. Let them begin to help you master your inner gremlin who is always trying to mess things up for you by causing problems and making mischief in your life. Let your animal clan guide demonstrate to you what they are here to show you, and help you reconnect with your true, higher self that is still living in the depths of your heart. Then, you can start removing from your life all mischief and heartache that your gremlin has created for you.

CHAPTER 11

THE POWER OF CHOICE

'The final forming of a person's character lies in their own hands.'
Anne Frank

So, you've done the test, identified your animal clan guide, read about your critical voice, the gremlin, and identified what tools can support you with your exam stress. You should be good to go. *But, are you?*

The tools you have read about in this book are only part of the possible solution. More importantly, the other part is your willingness to invest in yourself by taking responsibility for where you want to be. Sometimes, it is often easier to remain where you are because the enormity of this responsibility is just too much. Or it might be easier to do nothing and just carry on as you've always done because it takes too much effort. It might be none of those, perhaps you just don't know where or how to start. Well the answer is simple – start small and build it gradually. Each day, do one thing relating to your animal clan guide that will help you move from a helpless, stressed space into an empowered, motivated one.

We know how hard being a teenager is, with all those emotions whizzing around you. We know because we've also experienced it. It is a confusing time when you are exploring who you are. To add to this, you're also expected to sit these pesky exams and be what everyone else expects you to be, instead of whom you want to be. However, you are not alone.

Remember that this book is something you can pick up and easily access without wasting hours and hours of reading. It is just one way of supporting you and might give you an idea about your inner resources. It is not the only way, nor does it have all the answers. It's simply a guide to support you with your exams. There are many other books and ideas written by others on this subject, which we have included in the back of this book. All of these are an invitation for you to take positive steps. You can also get help from other organisations, or your parents, carers or teachers.

It is important for you to remind yourself that we all have different gifts and skills to share with others. However, the first step is recognising your gifts within yourself and accept who you are instead of rejecting parts of yourself you don't like. Remember that what you do to yourself, you invite the world to do to you too; therefore, don't reject you, but learn to celebrate you.

So, here are a few last minute emergency pointers. When you're feeling on the edge of panic and not being able to cope:

- Stop whatever it is you are doing.
- Belly breathing technique to centre yourself might help (see the appendices for method).
- Find a quiet place to sort through your thoughts.
- Decide which ones are true and which ones are not.
- Refer to this guide and your animal clan guide for some insight.
- Talk to someone responsible about how you're feeling, so you can get the support you need and deserve.

We hope that we have in some way managed to offer you some useful tools to support you on your journey and wish you all the very best with your exams and your life. We have also included some meditation and visualisation techniques at the back of this book to support you.

For more information about our services and workshops please go to our website: www.thelaidbackguidecompany.com

Wishing you all the very best,

Jennie Casewell and Naseem Ahsun

APPENDIX i

THE LAID BACK GUIDE QUESTIONNAIRE

THE LAID-BACK GUIDE QUIZ QUESTIONS

The quiz is for guidance only and is not a definitive means of defining who you are. It is only a guide inviting you to become more self-aware of yourself.

INSTRUCTIONS

The answers are relevant to how you have been most of your life and how you are now.

ONLY answer the ones that are **TRUE** statements about you by circling them. If it is only **SOMETIMES TRUE** to you, then **LEAVE IT OUT**.

REMEMBER the quiz is about **WHO YOU ARE** and not about what you want to be like.

A final word of caution: it is really important for you to be as honest with yourself as possible versus picking answers you feel will show you in a positive way, or reflect what you'd like to be like. That will **NOT** help you understand who you are. By being honest, you will get a better idea of who your animal clan guide is; therefore, you will receive the correct guidance and tools to support you when you are feeling stressed.

There are no good or bad answers, only honest ones. You can sit with friends or family whilst you're doing the test, as they probably know what you're like more than you do.

No animal clan guide type is better than another, as they each have their own unique and amazing gift.

The test should take you about 15-20 minutes.

1. I get fearful about making decisions, so I depend on others to help me make them.
2. Because I'm so relaxed and easy-going, people often lean on me for support and overwhelm me by asking me to do more than I can comfortably manage.
3. I am uniquely creative and I like being in environments that allow me to work in my own unique way.
4. I always look on the bright side of life because I'm an optimist.
5. I am a great friend who will always support you through difficult times, no matter how inconvenient it is for me.
6. I am a very private person and dislike it when others try to invade my privacy.
7. I am always focused on my goal and am constantly putting plans into action to achieve it.
8. I am always ready to defend myself.
9. I am easy-going, approachable and laid back.
10. I am intense and have strong, passionate emotions about my problems. I have to share them as it helps me come to a solution.
11. I am quite able to get on with things by myself and rarely need anyone's help. Actually, I prefer being left alone.
12. I enjoy being part of a group where I can fully participate and everybody is considered trustworthy and equal.
13. I am very considerate of others: especially, as I take the time to get to know what they like and dislike. I'd hate to upset them in anyway because I need their approval.

14. I believe that actions speak louder than words, so will wait to see whether people can be trusted to do what they say they are going to do.
15. I can be relied upon to complete most tasks to a high standard, and have high expectations of others and myself.
16. I can sense people's emotions even when they don't share them.
17. I can't sit still for very long because I get bored easily. I would rather be occupied with lots of different, fun-filled and interesting activities.
18. I don't like sharing personal information about myself.
19. I enjoy 'people watching' because their reactions fascinate me and I am able to learn more about how people act and behave.
20. I enjoy volunteering my time to help others without expecting anything back.
21. I don't like dwelling on negative emotions, as they ruin my potential to succeed.
22. I find it easier and simpler to go with the flow instead of making a fuss.
23. I hate being restricted by rules and regulations as it means I can't do what I want to do.
24. I hate making mistakes because perfection is the only thing that will do.
25. I have strong views and values, which I often express, especially when I'm right.
26. I know I need to take more notice of looking after myself instead of always focusing on looking after others.
27. I like to be considered as unusual because I love being unique.
28. I like to be admired for being the best at what I do.

29. I love being around others, and am considered the life of the party.
30. I love spontaneous and unplanned adventures because they are exciting. You're never quite sure what's going to happen.
31. I love working with facts and figures; actually, I'm really good at it because it is so logical and makes sense.
32. I need really clear instructions and guidelines, as I get anxious: especially if it involves something new or different.
33. I often fail to move in any direction because I get lost and confused by all the options in front of me.
34. I often feel that there is something wrong with me, when I compare myself to others.
35. I like to keep my distance and spend time on my own.
36. I often take the lead and give instructions.
37. I like being indispensible to my friends and colleagues.
38. Humour is a great way for helping me to lighten up and not feel so anxious.
39. I am very competitive and play to win.
40. I will jump into most situations where others are being bullied without thinking about the consequences, or my own safety.
41. I will spend ages gathering lots of knowledge about a subject, because I like others to consider me as intelligent, knowledgeable and capable.
42. I will work hard to maintain a peaceful environment by making sure everyone is relaxed and calm.
43. I'll always put in that extra effort to help others.
44. I'm always happy to help you, as long as it doesn't take up too much of my time and energy.

45. Others often misunderstand me, especially if they follow 'normal', mundane activities and are part of the 'in-crowd'.
46. I'm brutally honest, even when it upsets people. There's no point in tiptoeing around things, best to deal with things in a direct and straightforward way.
47. I'm considered strong and tough, so people avoid confrontations with me.
48. I'm really easy to get along with because I'm straightforward and uncomplicated: what you see is what you get.
49. I'm reluctant to put my views forward especially if it disturbs the peace. Sometimes, it's just easier to keep quiet and live a comfortable life.
50. I really enjoy producing perfect and imaginative work, but it has to look right.
51. I'm very outgoing and love the limelight where I can be noticed and receive attention.
52. It annoys me when others think it is ok to break the rules.
53. It annoys me when people can't control themselves by behaving properly, especially in public places, where others can judge them.
54. It really upsets me when people aren't as caring to me as I am to them, especially because of everything I do for them.
55. It's either right or wrong. Maybe doesn't exist.
56. I prefer living in my own world, which is comfortable, laid back and non-threatening.
57. Life is too short to focus on depressing things, so I try to avoid depressing situations as much as I can by distracting myself with fun activities.
58. Often I doubt myself; so go along with what others think, versus what my inner guide is telling me to do.

59. People are always sharing their problems with me because they know I am empathetic and understanding; therefore, they know I have a unique understanding of them and their problems.
60. People depend on me to protect them because they rely on my strength.
61. The secret to my success is that I can adapt my plans to meet my goals, especially if it means winning.
62. When I have to do something new or different, I will focus on all the possible things that can go wrong.
63. I'm great at getting myself noticed because I present an ambitious, successful image.

Having completed the test, work out your answers by putting a tick by the numbers you have circled in the test in the table below. Next calculate your answers by adding up the ticks and putting the number of ticks in the total column in the circle, e.g.

24 √	4	
25	17 √	
50	23	
52 √	29 √	
53	30 √	
55	44 √	
15 √	57	
3	4	
S	OT	

You might find that you have ticks in all the columns; this is because we all have an element of all the types in us. However, it is the column with the most ticks that will help you determine your animal clan guide. If you find that you have two columns that are equal, then read both chapters on that animal clan guide to determine which one you think you are.

24	4	8	1	2	3	5	6	21
25	17	36	12	9	10	13	11	28
50	23	40	14	22	16	20	18	39
52	29	46	32	33	27	26	19	51
53	30	47	38	42	34	37	31	61
55	44	48	58	49	45	43	35	63
15	57	60	62	56	59	54	41	7
S	OT	B	DR	O	W	D	T	L

S = Swan
OT =Otter

B = Bear
DR = Deer

O = Orangutan
W = Wolf

D = Dog
T = Tiger

L = Lioness

APPENDIX ii

PRACTICAL LAID BACK ACTIVITIES

In the sections, *'The Tools I Can Use to Deal with Exam Stress,'* we mentioned activities that would be beneficial for those with certain animal clan guides. This does not mean that they are exclusive to them at all. Whatever your animal clan guide, you are most welcome to try out these techniques too.

DISCLAIMER

Before we begin, we'd like to remind you that any exercises are suggested activities only. They are considered safe and designed as relaxing, motivating and de-stressing aids. In no way, do they replace medical or psychological treatment. If you have been diagnosed with a physical condition such as asthma or epilepsy, a disability or with a mental illness, then please consult with your parents, carers and health-care provider before trying any exercises in this chapter.

LAID BACK GUIDE AFFIRMATION CARDS

We have created a pack of animal clan guide affirmation cards designed to inspire you to access your inner resources. There is a set of eight affirmations per animal clan guide and each one will be relevant to you dependent on the situation. For more details, please visit our website: www.thelaidbackguidecompany.com

MEDITATION

WHAT IS MEDITATION?

Simply put, meditation is an ancient practice that helps you to enter a space, which is relaxed and calm. It can quiet the mental chatter of your mind and help to relieve stress. Things become clearer and calmer; especially if you've been lost in a fog.

It's free and easy to do, although you can also attend meditation classes if you prefer. It can take some practise to learn how to be comfortable sitting still and focusing your attention inwards, instead of on the noise and distractions around you. Don't worry if you find it difficult at first. It may take practice.

It's great to do first thing in the morning because it takes you to that calm state of mind and sets you up for the day. However, some of you might try this at night because it can help with winding down after a long day.

You can start off with doing just 3-5 minutes a day, in the morning and after you come back from school, then begin to build up over time to about 20 minutes.

Here are two simple methods for you to try:

BREATHING MEDITATION

Make sure you are wearing loose clothing and have taken your shoes off. It is best to also find a place where you won't be distracted, like your bedroom, or outside in the garden. Wherever it is, make sure you're not too warm or not too cold. Make sure ALL technological devices, like your cell phone, are switched off.

- Sit either on the floor cross-legged, or sit upright in a chair with your feet firmly connecting with the ground. If your feet can't touch the ground, then place a cushion or pillow under your feet.
- Next, take a moment to look around and notice where you are, and picture the details in your mind.
- Now, close your eyes and become aware of your breathing. Don't force your breath; just breathe, naturally. Be conscious of the air

coming in through your nostrils and out through your mouth. Feel the air as it fills your lungs when you inhale, and deflates them when you exhale.

- At first, you will be very distracted because it seems the noise, distractions and chatter have become worse, but this is not the case. It is just that you are becoming aware of exactly how noisy and busy your mind is.
- If you find yourself becoming distracted, then don't worry about it; just refocus your thoughts on your breathing again.
- Finally, when you're ready to come out of your meditation, simply visualise where you are again. Wriggle your fingers and toes, and then open your eyes.

You might find that in your first few attempts, you are only able to focus on your breath for a moment or two. But please don't give up because it is like learning to walk. It takes one step at a time. The more you practise, the better you will become at it.

GROUNDING MEDITATION

Grounding simply means connecting with your physical environment. Sometimes, when we're stressed and full of fear, we can become confused and disconnected from reality and our higher self. By grounding, you help yourself reconnect to the here and now, your higher self and what is real, versus what is imagined.

Again, make sure you're wearing loose clothing and your technology is switched off. Find somewhere quiet where you won't be disturbed, like your room, or the garden.

- Sit either on the floor cross-legged, or sit upright in a chair with your feet firmly connecting with the ground. If your feet can't touch the ground, then place a cushion or pillow under you feet.

- Next, take a moment to look around and notice where you are, and picture the details in your mind.
- Now close your eyes and become aware of your breathing. As you inhale through your nostrils, follow your breath down into your lungs and focus on how it settles around your navel and allows your belly to expand. Spend a few minutes focusing on your breath in this way and your energy on your navel. You might even begin to feel a pulse around your navel area, which is an indicator of your level of focus.
- Next, become aware of your feet on the floor or cushion. Imagine roots growing out of them and moving down past the building and connecting deep into the earth.
- As you feel the connection between you and the earth grow stronger, imagine the earth sending its own energy through the roots to energise and sustain you. Focus your attention here for as long as you can.
- When you are ready, feel the roots begin to retract back into your feet and allow your awareness to move back up through your legs to your navel, then further up connecting with your breath and the rest of your body.
- Have a picture of your room in your mind's eye and wriggle your fingers and toes to bring you back. When you are ready, open your eyes.
- Take a few moments to readjust yourself before getting on with your day, or evening.

BELLY BREATHING FOR CENTRING AND CALMING YOUR NERVES

Here's a quick easy technique, which might help you calm your nerves just before you walk into your exam. It's also one to use whenever you feel an onset of stress getting the better of you.

- Imagine you're fed up and let out a sigh releasing all the air in your lungs. Imagine your shoulders relaxing and your muscles loosen.
- Now you're ready to take a breath in slowly. As you breathe in deeply, feel you stomach expand as the air fills it. Do this to a count of approximately 5 seconds – don't worry, if you can't – do it as close to 5 seconds as you can.
- Now release your breath to the count of 5 seconds (or as close as) and feel your muscles relax even more.
- Repeat this 3 times.
- Repeat, if necessary.

VISUALISATION

Visualisation is a quick and easy technique, which can support you in achieving the outcome you want. Athletes have successfully used it for years to motivate themselves to achieve their goals. It's about using your mind to imagine a positive outcome for yourself, using all five senses – sight, smell, hearing, taste, touch. With practise, you can hold that image in your mind, particularly when you feel down or stressed. It is there to motivate you to persevere through your challenges and achieve your goal.

To build your image, do the following:

- First, make sure you are somewhere quiet where you won't be disturbed. Don't forget to turn your technology, or cell phone, off.
- Take a moment to notice everything around you.
- Now close your eyes. You're ready to visualise results day and getting your results.
- Begin with what you can see. What are you wearing? Where are you? Who are you with? What time of day is it? What's the weather like?

- Next, what can you hear?
- What can you smell? What does your mouth taste and feel like?
- Finally, imagine yourself collecting your results and opening them. Visualise the grades you want, sparkling off of the page.
- How are you feeling now?
- Hold onto that wonderful feeling as you imagine yourself back in your present location. Ground yourself by wriggling your fingers and toes. When you're ready, open your eyes.

CREATING A VISION BOARD

If you'd like something more concrete and permanent, then there is nothing better than creating your own vision board, full of things you want to achieve, especially with your exams. It can be as unique, creative and detailed as you would like it to be. All you will need is a mini corkboard and some pins – these can be found easily at office stores.

Your vision board might include anything, like: pictures, quotes, great comments from your teachers about you and your work, song lyrics, affirmations from your animal clan guide, a picture of your animal clan guide (not just from the book, but perhaps in its natural habitat). You could write a poem about your dreams and aspirations, basically, anything that can motivate you and support you throughout your exams.

Remember to have your board someplace you'll see it. Make it the first thing you wake up to in the morning to remind you of all that you really are.

HATHA YOGA

Simply put, Hatha Yoga is the physical aspect of Yoga. It involves a set of physical movements (asanas or poses) which are designed to help you connect with your breath and body. By doing slow, almost stretching-like exercises, it helps you to unite your mind and body and bring them into balance.

There are several DVDs out there, as well as classes you can attend. However, with any form of exercise do check with your health-care provider first.

WHITE NOISE

White noise is actually static sound, which sounds like a gentle hiss in the background and has been said to help relaxation, focus and restful sleep. White noise CDs and machines are readily available. Search for more details on the Internet.

IDEAS FOR GROUP QUIZ GAMES - MAKE STUDYING FUN.

The following well-known quiz games can be adapted to support your study group activities. They are fun, motivating and give you an opportunity to test yourselves and your friends.

WORD ASSOCIATION GAME

This is a variation on a well-known game where you have a time limit to describe a concept or idea linked to a topic you are studying without naming the topic.

This can be done in two teams and requires a minimum of four people. You need to give yourself a time, like two minutes to describe as many topics as possible to your team. Write the topics on pieces of paper, fold them up and place them in a bag.

For example – if you are studying for Biology, you would have to create a list of topics first on pieces of paper e.g. photosynthesis, hormones, heart and respiratory system.

- The person, whose turn it is, might pick a topic out of the bag like, photosynthesis and will have a maximum of two minutes to describe it without saying the name.
- The rule is that they can only use words to describe it. DON'T mime, or act it out. If the team get it within the time, then they win a point.
- If the team is still within the time limit, then they can have a go at guessing another topic.
- If they don't manage to get it, then the other team has a chance to steal the point by having a go at guessing.

You can also use this game to help with English (e.g. language or poetry techniques), History (e.g. important dates), Geography (e.g. geographical terms) or Maths (e.g. ratios, fractions).

CHARADES

This is an old family favourite that has been around for a long time. Again, this involves teams and can be used for a number of subjects and topics. It involves two groups, with each member taking turns in picking a topic and miming it to their team. They, in turn, have to guess what it is. Just write your topics on pieces of paper. Fold it and put it in a hat/bag, so people can't see the topics they are choosing. Remember you can also agree a time limit between you (e.g. five minutes might be a realistic time-frame).

There are some generic mimes to indicate what type of text it is for example:

- Open hands means it is a book.
- Holding one closed hand to your eye and doing a clockwise camera motion with the other means it's a film.
- Opening your arms wide as if you're welcoming people or about to hug them, means it is a play.
- To make it more fun, you could make up other mime motions related to subjects. For example, for chemistry, you can mime pretending to hold the test tube and swirling it. For Geography, you can mime reading a map. Use your imagination and make it fun.

For example: if you're studying English and a Shakespeare play like, *'Romeo and Juliet'*.

- Pick the team member who'll go first.
- They pick up a topic.

- Then mime it. Remember you have a time limit of about five minutes, or whatever you've decided it will be.
- They can either mime all of it, or part of it, or a word at time.
- So you might want to mime the death of Romeo and Juliet at the end of the play to help your teammates get the right answer. Decide and select the most effective information, or key words to mime.

TWENTY QUESTIONS

This is a variation of a very well known family game created in the US. Each person takes a turn at being the answerer. They choose a topic, which other players have twenty questions in which to guess. The answerer can only answer "Yes or No". If the others do not get the topic right, then the answerer gets to stay in that position for another round.

So, if your group study session is for Physics, Business Studies or Maths, then the game needs to be based on that. Or you can break it down even more to sub-topics within the subject, dependent on what your group study session is about.

BINGO

This is a great game to play and create if you're studying any languages. All you need are a few resources, including creating a 4 x 4 or 5 x 5 bingo card table e.g.

You could create your own blank bingo sheet and then the group could decide on some topics for your subject (e.g. French or Spanish could be days of the week, months and numbers) which you then fill with a choice of these topics.

- Decide on a quiz master, who will then randomly read out days of the week, months and numbers in either: French, Spanish, Mandarin or whatever language you are studying.
- As the quiz master reads the answers out in that language, check to see whether you have written them down and cross them off if you have.
- The first player to get a line, either horizontal or vertical, wins.

JEOPARDY

This is a variation on a well-known quiz game where players are presented with answers as clues and they have to form the answers as appropriate questions. For example, a clue might be – add the numbers in the list together then divide by the amount of numbers in the list. The player would be given this clue and would formulate their answer as a question. In this instance, the answer would be - How do you calculate the mean? You've guessed it; the topic is Maths and averages.

This game requires a bit of pre-planning, as you have to come up with the clues and designated topics prior to the session. So, it might be something the group can do before meeting up for the study session. If you can each create ten or twenty clues each, then you can each take turns in becoming the quiz master.

These are just some ideas, which can help you with fun, focused group study session.

BIBLIOGRAPHY

Andrews, T. (2010). *Animal Speak: The Spiritual & Magical Powers of Creatures Great and Small.* US: Llewellyn Publications.

Berne, E. (2009). *Games People Play: The Psychology of Human Relationships.* UK: Penguin Books.

Carlini, J. (2014). *Maximizing Your Enneagram Type a workbook: Improve Your Life by Identifying, Understanding, and Developing Your Strengths.* UK: John Carlini.

Carson, R. D. (2003). *Taming Your Gremlin.* US: HarperCollins.

Chestnut, B. (2013). T*he Complete Enneagram: 27 Paths to Greater Self-Knowledge.* US: She Writes Press.

Craig, H. (2014). *Recognizing The Enneagram: Do Not Just Be Content With Being Yourself - Discover The Better You.* US: CreateSpace Independent Publishing Platform.

Daniels, D. N. and Price, V. (2009). *The essential Enneagram.* US: HarperOne.

Farmer, S. (2006). *Animal Spirit Guides: An Easy-to-Use Handbook for Identifying and Understanding Your Power Animals and Animal Spirit Helpers.* UK: Hay House.

---. (2009). *Power Animals: How to Connect with Your Animal Spirit Guide.* US: Hay House.

Fitzel, R. (2015) *The Nine Types of Students.* Available at: http://www.fitzel.ca/enneagram/education/index.html (Accessed: Sept 2015).

Freed, A. M. and Faul-Jansen, R. (1976) *T.A. for Teens and Other Important People* (Transactional Analysis for Everybody Series; 5th). US: Jalmar Pr.

Keyes, M. F. (1991). *Enneagram Relationship Workbook: A Self and Partnership Assessment Guide.* US: Molysdatur Pubns.

---. (1992). *Emotions and the Enneagram: Working Through Your Shadow Life Script*. US: Molysdatur Pubns.

Harris, A. B. and Harris, T. (1995). *Staying Ok*. UK: Arrow.

Holden, C. (2013). *Strokes and Hungers* (Transactional Analysis in Bite Sized Chunks) [ebook]. Accessed: from Amazon.com

---. (2013). *The Ego States* (Transactional Analysis in Bite Sized Chunks Book 1) [ebook]. Accessed: from Amazon.com

---. (2013). *The Drama Triangle* (Transactional Analysis in Bite Sized Chunks Book 2) [ebook]. Accessed: from Amazon.com

Horsley, M. (2005). *The Enneagram for the Spirit: How to Make Peace with Your Personality and Understand Others*. US: Barron's Educational Series..

Howe-Murphy, R. (2013). *Deep Living: Transforming Your Relationship to Everything That Matters Through the Enneagram*. US: Enneagram Press.

Hurley, K. (2012). *Discover Your Soul Potential: Using the Enneagram to Awaken Spiritual Vitality*. US: CreateSpace Independent Publishing Platform.

Hurley, K. V. and Dobson, T. E. (1992). *What's My Type?* US: HarperOne.

---. (1993). *My Best Self: Using the enneagram to free the soul*. US: HarperOne.

James, M. (1974). *Transactional Analysis for Moms and Dads*. US: Addison-wesley.

Joines, V. and Steward, I. (2002). *Personality Adaptations: A New Guide to Human Understanding in Psychotherapy and Counseling*. UK: Lifespace Pub.

---. (2012). *Ta Today: A New Introduction to Transactional Analysis*. UK: Vann Joines.

Jongeward, D. & James, M. (2008). *Born To Win: Transactional Analysis With Gestalt Experiments.* US: Da Capo Press.

Keyes, J. (2002). *Guide to Natural Health: Using the Horoscope as a Key to Ancient Healing Practices.* US: Llewellyn Publications.

Lapid-Bogda, G. (2009). *Bringing Out the Best in Everyone You Coach.* US: McGraw-Hill Education.

Lapworth, P. (2011). *An Introduction to Transactional Analysis: Helping People Change.* UK: SAGE Publications Ltd.

Levin, P. (1988). *Becoming the Way We Are: An Introduction to Personal Development in Recovery and in Life.* US: Health Communications.

Levine, J. (1999). *The Enneagram Intelligences: Understanding Personality for Effective Teaching and Learning.* US: Praeger

Linden, A. (1994). *The Enneagram and NLP: A Journey of Evolution.* US: Metamorphous Press.

Mellor, E. (2004). *Teen Stages: How to Guide the Journey to Adulthood.* Australia: Finch Publishing.

Mellor, K. (2009). *Teen Stages: The Breakthrough Year-by-Year Approach to Understanding Your Ever-Changing Teen.* Australia: Sourcebooks, Inc.

---. (2012). *Inspiration Meditation & Personal Wellbeing: A Practical Guide to Balanced Living.* Australia: The Awakening Network Inc.

Meyer, R. (2015). *Animal Messengers: An A-Z Guide to Signs and Omens in the Natural World.* US: Bear & Company.

Pollack, J. (2014). *Knowing me knowing them* [ebook]. Accessed: from Amazon.com

Rhodes, S. (2009). *The Positive enneagram a new approach to the nine personality types.* [ebook]. Accessed: from Amazon.com

Riso, D. R., 1996. *Personality Types: Using the Enneagram for Self-Discovery.* US: Mariner Books.

---. (1999). *The Wisdom of the Enneagram: The Complete Guide to Psychological and Spiritual Growth for the Nine Personality Types.* US: Bantam.

Smith, J. W. (2011). *The Enneagram Types and Tips for Happiness: Specific, practical tips for happiness for each personality type.* UK: CreateSpace Idependent Publishing Platform.

---. (2012). *How to Create a Happier Life with the Enneagram: Process Exercises.* UK: Wells-Smith Partners.

Steiner, C. (1994). *Scripts People Live: Transactional Analysis of Life Scripts.* US: Grove Press.

Stewart, I. (1989). *Transactional Analysis Counselling in Action* (Counselling in Action series).UK: SAGE Publications Ltd.

The Enneagram Institute. Accessed: Sept 2015, http://www.enneagraminstitute.com

Tudor, K. (2002). *Transactional Analysis Approaches to Brief Therapy: What do you say between saying hello and goodbye?* (Brief Therapies series). UK: SAGE Publications Ltd.

Wagele, E. (1997). *The Enneagram of Parenting: The 9 Types of Children and How to Raise Them Successfully.* US: HarperOne.

---. (2014). *The Enneagram for Teens: Discover Your Personality Type and Celebrate Your True Self.* US: Pli media

Wagner, J.(2005). *An Introduction to the Enneagram: Personality Styles and Where You Fit.* US: MJF Books, Fine Communications.

---. (2010). *Nine Lenses on the World: the Enneagram Perspective.* US: Enneagram Studies and Applications.

Widdowson, M. (2009). *Transactional Analysis: 100 Key Points and Techniques.* UK:Routledge.

REFERENCES

Nspcc.org.uk. (2015). *Under Pressure Childline Review.* (p.51) Available at: https://www.nspcc.org.uk/globalassets/documents/annual-reports/childline-review-under-pressure.pdf. (Accessed:15 November 2015).

Oxford University Press. (2015). *'Gremlin'.* Available at: www.oxforddictionaries.com. (Accessed: 21 August 2015).

CPSIA information can be obtained
at www.ICGtesting.com
Printed in the USA
BVOW11s1405220316
441312BV00006B/19/P